A Clarion Call
to
Protect Your Home

In a World at Enmity with God and the
Family He Loves

E Bruce & Marina Evans
33131 Monroy Circle
Temecula, CA   92592

A Clarion Call
to
Protect Your Home

In a World at Enmity with God and the Family He Loves

MARCELO A. TOLOPILO

Includes
The Duties of Parents
by J. C. Ryle

Edited by Marcelo A. Tolopilo

Chart & Compass Press
Temecula, California

A Clarion Call to Protect Your Home
In a World at Enmity with God and the Family He Loves

Copyright © 2008 by Marcelo A. Tolopilo

Published by Chart & Compass Press
www.chartandcompasspress.com

Scripture quotations taken from the New American Standard Bible®,
Copyright © 1960, 1962, 1963, 1968, 1971, 1972, 1973, 1975, 1977, 1995 by The
Lockman Foundation. Used by permission. (www.Lockman.org).

The Duties of Parents
by J. C. Ryle

Copyright © 2008 edited by Marcelo A. Tolopilo

Scripture quotations are from The Holy Bible, English Standard Version®,
copyright © 2001 by Crossway Bibles, a publishing ministry of Good News
publishers. Used by permission. All rights reserved.

Cover design and typesetting by Silver Lion Designs Co. (silverliondesign.com)

To report errors, please send a note to errors@chartandcompasspress.com.

ISBN 978-0-9821032-0-3

Printed by Jostens in the United States of America

WATCH MOTHER

Mother! Watch the little feet
Climbing o'er the garden wall,
Bounding through the busy street,
Ranging cellar, shed and hall,
Never count the moments lost,
Never count the time it costs;
Little feet will go astray;
Guide them, mother while you may.

Mother! Watch the little hand
Picking berries by the way,
Making houses in the sand,
Tossing up the fragrant hay,
Never dare the question ask,
"Why to me this weary task?"
These same little hands may prove
Messengers of light and love.

Mother! Watch the little tongue
Prattling, eloquent and wild,
What is said, and what is sung
By the happy, joyous child.
Catch the word while yet unspoken.
Stop the vow before 'tis broken;
This same tongue may yet proclaim
Blessings in a Saviour's name.

Mother! Watch the little heart
Beating soft and warm for you;
Wholesome lessons now impart;
Keep, O keep that young heart true,
Extracting every bitter weed,
Sowing good and precious seed;
Harvest rich you then may see,
Ripening for eternity.

Contents

Preface

Christian parents – of whom I am one – have the great call and privilege to protect their homes, and in that environment lead their children to the Savior, and disciple them for godly living. Truly, the magnificent venture of the Great Commission (evangelism and discipleship, Matthew 28:18-20) begins at home. People need to see that Jesus Christ changes lives. For many, the primary evidence of Christ's transforming message is the metamorphosis He brings to our families. Our call to protect and guide our homes is foundational to the Christian enterprise.

Yet, the frequent frenzy of life, the fallen world in which we live, and our unredeemed flesh conspire to draw us away from this great parental purpose. It is my sincere hope and earnest prayer that this humble volume will remind us of, and draw us back to this supreme objective of Christian parenting.

In this book, I briefly address three important areas where the Christian family is under assault: the marriage union, the parent/child relationship, and the innocence of our children. I draw practical attention to these battlefronts with two extended application sections designed to strengthen the marriage relationship and the parenting endeavor. I trust these exercises will prove helpful to the reader.

I have also appealed to the wise and godly advice of one of the great pastoral voices of the last one and a half centuries, J. C. Ryle. His seventeen insightful parenting principles alone will reward your investment in this book.

I am presently working on a broader work that builds on the principles put forth in this publication. Barring a promotion to heaven, it should be released in 2009.

CHAPTER ONE

The Increasing Hostility of the World Toward God and the Family

We live in a postmodern world. Western culture, and of particular interest to us, American secular culture has moved beyond the certainties of the modern era and embraced the ludicrous insanity of relativistic subjectivism. The intellectual elite – particularly the pseudo-sages of higher education and the media – have convinced the masses that it is sophisticated and beneficial to abandon objective truth, reject rules, and live by one's intuition.

"Truth is relative" is the ever growing mantra of our culture. The late Allan Bloom, philosopher and professor at the University of Chicago, addressed this very issue among college students of his day. In his perceptive book "The Closing of The American Mind," Dr. Bloom recognized the ubiquitous nature of relativism among young people, the visceral fervor with which they clung to it, and the abject contempt they felt for those who didn't. Since Dr. Bloom wrote his book, relativism has only metastasized and become the ingrained orthodoxy of our culture. In 1987 Dr. Bloom reflected,

"The relativity of truth is not a theoretical insight but a moral postulate, the condition of a free society, or so [the students] see it. They have all been equipped with this framework early on, and it is the modern replacement for the inalienable natural rights that used to be the traditional American grounds for a free society. That it is a moral issue for students is revealed by the character of their response when challenged - a combination of disbelief and indignation: "Are you an absolutist?" the only alternative they know, uttered in the same tone as "Are you a monarchist?" or "Do you really believe in witches?"[1]

Objective realities embraced by our founding forefathers, such as the existence of God, and the supreme and singular value of the Bible in shaping our national thought, conscience, and behavior, have been generally rejected as relics of an outmoded and failed system of thought. We have largely abandoned the moral moorings of Judeo-Christian belief for an epistemological narcissism: the idea that each person must determine what is true for them and act in their own best interest.

I don't believe we have slid down the relativistic moral slope as much as other western countries, but we are certainly making haste to catch up. Our culture has increasingly rejected God's laws written on the heart (Romans 2:15), and as a consequence we have - to the degree we have slipped - been given over to, and deluded by, an anti-biblical way of thinking and the subsequent debauched, godless value system it produces.

It is no surprise to any Christian that this postmodern framework is antithetical to God's pattern for the family. In fact, it rages and rails against it. A culture that incrementally detaches itself from righteousness and justice will by default attack the institutions God has ordained, including the family.

This is why the basic unit of society, a "nuclear family" (i.e., a man and wife with their own dependent children) lies in virtual ruin today. It has been blasted from pillar to post by moral relativism, and divorce. In the secular arena, finding a traditional family untouched by the ravages of sexual sin and, or divorce is practically an anomaly. Whereas two generations ago the traditional family formed the norm in our country, today it is an endangered institution. The family is under siege. The destructive influences of our culture have hit their mark with predictable devastation.

Please understand, I do not believe there is a vast left-wing conspiracy against the institution of the home. Where we are today is the natural and tragic outworking of a God-rejecting, truth-rejecting culture.

When men choose to ignore God's evident design for society, the influence of biblical thought, and their God-given conscience, God in turn gives them over to their fallen understanding, the resulting behavior, and the terrible consequences of their actions (Romans 1:18-ff). This certainly applies in the arena of the home. The prevalent chaos in the modern family is simply the temporal wrath of God unleashed on those who repeatedly reject Him, and His pattern for familial health and stability.

Obviously scripture teaches that all "unbelieving" men are hostile to God (Romans 5:10; Romans 8:7; Ephesians 2:1-3; Colossians 1:21). Unbelief equals hostility to some degree - as Paul reminds us in Romans 8:7, "because the mind set on the flesh is hostile toward God." Furthermore, all degrees of unbelief are ultimately, spiritually, and eternally lethal. That said, there are levels of hostility.

There is such a thing as progressive unbelief with its corresponding hostility to truth. Romans one implicitly teaches that. Not all men or cultures have rejected truth to the extent of divine abandonment we read about in Romans chapter one. America was not as hostile to a Judeo-Christian ethic at its founding, or in the years following the Great Awakening, as it is today.

However, the more a person or a culture rejects the truth, the more hostile they become to the truth, to the God of truth, and to people who love to practice the truth. When I say that we are a "post-modern" culture, I mean that we have progressively abandoned objective truth, particularly divine revelation (in nature - Romans 1:19, 20; inscribed on our conscience - Romans 2:15, and of course in God's written word). Indeed, we have become post-Christian in our outlook.

Modern man asserts that all truth, and especially spiritual truth, is unknowable. He rejects God's standard, and in its place he establishes the individual and his subjective opinions as the arbiter of right and wrong, good and evil. When man's fallen reason reigns, one thing is certain: he will turn God's value system upside down and inside out. Evil becomes good, and good evil, as men "substitute darkness for light and light for darkness, who substitute bitter for sweet and sweet for bitter" (Isaiah 5:20). The result: man ends up following and living a lie.

In short, because our culture has willfully and increasingly rejected God's revelation, we (the collective American 'we') have become incrementally hostile to God's ways and therefore antagonistic to the values He prescribes and the institutions He ordains and nurtures. Our culture is attacking and destroying some of the very systems that have contributed significantly to America's greatness, specifically marriage and the family. While this is not a conspiracy of any one group, it is the inevitable reality of an ever hostile, secular way of thinking.

From the beginning of creation, the family has been of primary importance to God. The family played and plays a critical role in the outworking of God's most glorious undertaking, the redemption of mankind! Directly after man's ruinous fall in the garden, God promised to send a redeemer to rescue man from sin and its consequences. This He promised to accomplish within the context of a family, the seed of woman, that is, a mother's son.

As such, He chose Abraham's family and promised, "For I have chosen him, so that he may command his children and his household after him to keep the way of the LORD by doing righteousness and justice, so that the LORD may bring upon Abraham what He has spoken about him," i.e., redemption to the nations of the earth (Genesis 18:18; 22:18; 26:4).

Within the families of Abraham, God continued His redemptive plan through the clan of Judah, and more specifically through the family of Jesse, then David, and all the way down the family tree to the righteous young family of Joseph and Mary who issued forth the Messiah of Israel and the Savior of the world.

God worked His redemptive promises through families until He realized His plan in the Lord Jesus Christ. And still, to this day, families are an important platform on which God stages the saving gospel. This is why Paul encouraged women to keep a godly home, "so that the word of God will not be dishonored" (Titus 2:5). Indeed, the family is infinitely precious to God. Since this is so, we should expect warfare on the family, especially given the growing hostility of our culture to what God esteems.

We must be spiritually alert and biblically discerning so that we might protect our families from the onslaught of the enemy. Please understand, the family, your family is under siege by a hostile enemy working through a culture at enmity with God and what He loves. We need to keep a vigilant eye open and our Bibles at the ready because you and I are in a battle for the spiritual wellbeing of our homes.

The Family Under Siege

My primary purpose in this brief book is to **alert you** to some of the crucial fronts on which our families face attack, as well the means by which these assaults are perpetrated. I fear we (Christians) have a tendency to acclimate, like the proverbial frog in the increasingly hot pot, to the rising heat of godward hostility in our culture. We often fail to recognize the world's hatred for God and the virtues and institutions He loves. We can grow used to the evil of our age without much vexation.

We forget we are engaged in a real war between God's Kingdom and the present world system, and specifically as it concerns this book, a conflict that rages over the survival of our families. If we are unaware of the dangers facing us, we will certainly fail to instruct and protect our homes accordingly.

The world system - consisting of unsaved humanity influenced and directed by "the prince of the power of the air" (Ephesians 2:2), "the god of this world" (2 Corinthians 4:4), Satan, is at war with the home - not just the Christian home, but the God-ordained institution of the home. The enemy is out to demolish the family as a whole, and while he takes special aim at the Christian family because of the critical role it plays in God's economy, his desire is to sabotage and destroy the family unit, society's most vital building block. With the family undermined and redefined, he is free to reshape society and its value system to reflect his opposition to God, and God's gracious plan for mankind.

To accomplish his malevolent work he attacks the family on several fronts. I would like to focus on three primary battlefields where he vents his destructive fury with great success in our present day. These three axes of conflict are the marriage union, the parent/child relationship, and the innocence of children. Before we contemplate some of the offensive means through which the enemy executes his destructive plan, let's consider these three critical theatres of war against the family.

CHAPTER TWO

The World's Assault on the Marriage Union

Obviously, Satan strives to destroy families by targeting the crucial relationship between husband and wife. The importance of the marriage union and the particular struggles men and women face have been written about at great length. There are some marvelous resources to which I would direct your attention if you desire to further strengthen your marriage (see references at the end of this section, "Biblical Resources for Marriage").

My purpose presently is to alert you - by way of reminder – to the singular reality that your relationship with your spouse is the object of a cosmic struggle. The apostle Peter warned us to be watchful for the wiles of the devil because the enemy of our souls is committed to our destruction. He wrote, "Be of sober spirit, be on the alert. Your adversary, the devil, prowls around like a roaring lion, seeking someone to devour" (1 Peter 5:8).

That verse does not specifically mention marriage, but the application of this biblical principle to the marriage union is obvious. If the devil can destroy your marriage, he will devour your family. Suffice it to say, if the marriage union between a man and a woman is sabotaged, the disintegration of the family generally follows in corresponding measure. Violation of marriage vows and the dissolution that frequently follows shatters families.

As a whole we have been desensitized to the devastating effects of ongoing marital conflict and divorce. This is especially true regarding divorce. Regrettably, annulment has become an acceptable risk of marriage to many, and it is frequently touted as a viable solution for a difficult relationship.

Sometimes I have heard troubled couples (even Christian couples) rationalize, "You know it's better if we go our separate ways. All we do when we're together is fight, and that is so harmful for the kids. My spouse and I are happier, better people and parents when we're not together, and that's just healthier for our entire family."

No one can deny that constant conflict is detrimental to the family. We would do well to follow Paul's exhortation to the Romans in our spousal relationship: "Let love be without hypocrisy. Abhor what is evil; cling to what is good. Be devoted to one another in brotherly love; give preference to one another in honor" (Romans 12:9, 10).

The hardest and best thing is to face the difficulties in a marriage relationship and to deal with them biblically. The easiest, short-term escape is to follow the path of least resistance, to ignore the challenges and abandon a relationship psychologically, or even physically, yet to do so brings devastating consequences that far outweigh the fleeting relief separation sometimes brings.

Make no mistake about it, to disavow your altar covenant and allow yourself to become emotionally separated from your life partner, or to seek an annulment of the marriage union is like setting off an emotional bomb in the lives of those you love. It will devastate your family, negatively impact your children and grandchildren, and further emasculate your gospel testimony.

Sin is like that, my friend. Unlike a surgical instrument that precisely cuts away tissue, sin is savage in its effect, much like an explosion. Sin shatters, tears, and shreds leaving a large swath of irreparable collateral damage in its destructive wake. The enemy through this world system is out to destroy the marriage union because if he does he brings devastation and chaos to the home, to society, and desolation to the believing household.

If Satan succeeds in bringing ruin to the Christian family, he compromises their testimony and rains untold grief upon their lives, producing one of the greatest and saddest ironies on this earth: defeated, joyless, silent Christians.

I realize that my point in this section is to simply yell, "Beware! Your marriage relationship has a target on it!", but allow me a pastoral moment to spur you on with a brief word of exhortation. My dear fellow Christian, be committed to your marriage, and be in prayer for your marriage. It is, as I said, the object of spiritual attack.

And the chief manner in which the enemy finds his destructive way into a marriage is through selfishness, i.e., looking out for your own interests first instead of those of your spouse. Secondly, and closely linked to selfishness, the enemy compromises many marriages through bitterness, a failure to forgive one another as we have been forgiven by God in Christ. As someone has well said, "Bitterness is the only poison we, ourselves, take hoping to make someone else sick." Selfishness and bitterness are deadly toxins to a marriage that will kill a relationship unless they are flushed out of the system and replaced by the sweet waters of God's truth and understanding.

The antidote to these woes, and many other acrimonious attitudes, is to pursue Christ-likeness, to immerse yourselves in the truths of Philippians 2:1-11 (selfless living), and Ephesians 5:21-33 (God's pattern for marriage mirrored in Christ's relationship to the church). Follow the example of your Savior and Master, the Lord Jesus.

Make the focal point of change yourself, not your spouse. Entrust the changes they need to make to the Lord. I realize that marriage struggles can be exceedingly difficult, but they are not beyond God's power to reform, nor the pain they inflict beyond the reach of God's hand to heal as we submit to His word. The marriage union is precious to God and worthy of our greatest efforts to protect and restore. If we don't, we are choosing to surrender our families to the schemes of the enemy.

Fight the good fight. Immerse yourself in the scriptures mentioned above, memorize them preferably together, study them carefully, understand them, and submit yourselves to the life-changing yoke of scripture. Invite God's Spirit to apply these truths to your heart at the point of need, and allow God Almighty to transform your lives and union. I implore you to battle with God's provision for your marriage. It will be difficult, but you will never regret the resulting work of God's grace in your home.

Another key battlefront for the family in today's context focuses on the crucial relationship between parents and their children. We will consider this in the upcoming chapter, but before we do please think about undertaking, or at least reading through the following two exercises designed to strengthen your marriage.

Fortifying Your Relationship

The first and continuous action you must take for the restoration and/or ongoing health of your marriage is this…

Bow your knee and PRAY (1 Thessalonians 5:17)

1) Ask God to reveal to you areas of selfishness and bitterness that have wounded, or alienated your spouse.

Continually search your heart for roots of selfishness and bitterness toward your covenant partner. Be honest with yourself and your Lord, and pray that God would reveal sin as it sprouts in your heart.

Remember the words of King David in Psalm 19:12-14, "Who can discern his errors? Acquit me of hidden faults. Also keep back Your servant from presumptuous sins; let them not rule over me; then I will be blameless, and I shall be acquitted of great transgression. Let the words of my mouth and the meditation of my heart be acceptable in Your sight, O LORD, my rock and my Redeemer." And also in Psalm 139:23, 24 David says, "Search me, O God, and know my heart; try me and know my anxious thoughts; and see if there be any hurtful way in me, and lead me in the everlasting way."

2) Personal repentance – Confess your sins to the Lord. Regardless of who you believe is "the greater sinner" in your relationship, ask God to forgive you of your sins, and ask your life partner to forgive you as well.

3) Ask God to give you compassion for your spouse. The only way to truly understand compassion is to remember that we have received it. So remember you yourself have transgressed against God who is absolutely holy (no one can sin in like manner against us because we are born sinners and behave as sinners), yet in His fathomless grace He has shown you great compassion. Pray the Lord would conceive a God-wrought compassion in your heart for your life partner.

4) Pray for the power to forgive. Remember two simple realities. First, we are all sinners and each one of us has fallen far short of being a perfect spouse. Two, Jesus Christ had to bear your moral failures (sins) on the cross so that you might be forgiven. You are infinitely indebted to Him because He forgave you a debt you could not pay, and He asks you to forgive those who have sinned against you.

5) Pray that God would protect your union from the evil that is working against your marriage in this world.

6) Ask God to make your marriage a trophy of His grace to your children, your family, and for the world to see.

7) Pray that the Lord would enable you to live out your biblical role within your marriage relationship.

8) Ask the Holy Spirit to give you understanding into the truths of marriage contained in His word.

As you're praying... **Study God's blueprint for your marriage relationship in His Book.**

I have included a couple of biblical exercises intended to help you discover God's mind for your marriage relationship. Both will take a time commitment from you, but there are no shortcuts to good marriages, or solving marriage difficulties. If you can, I would suggest you do both exercises, but at least start with one, with a mind to meet with the Lord through the pages of scripture.

If possible, I suggest you do these exercises concurrently with your spouse (independently of one another, and then coming together to talk about what you've discovered), but if that is not likely, pursue these exercises on your own, asking the Lord to change you and to make you the Christian, and spouse He would have you become.

A Word About Understanding Your Bible

One of the most powerful habits Christians must develop is the simple straightforward reading of God's word. Don't underestimate the power of the Bible to transform – to bring salvation to a lost soul, or to change the heart and habits of believers. However, in order for scripture to have its life altering effect, we must first understand what it means, and in order to understand it properly we must allow the word of God to speak for itself.

I have found that the honest (sans personal, cultural biases), humble, prayerful, observant, Spirit dependent, repeated reading of a text will unfold the objective meaning of God's word to you like few things can, and it is that truth – and that truth alone – that can change our lives. If we miss the forthright, objective meaning of a text, we deny ourselves the life changing power of the word. The Bible is not a lucky charm. Carrying one in your tote bag, or robotically reading favorite portions, or imbuing it with mystical meaning will not help you and your relationships. The power of the Bible is in its meaning. Without the true sense of it, we cannot apply it to our lives.

So, don't read into the text what you desire it to mean. Instead, let the words of scripture stand alone to mean what God intended them to mean in their historical (the time and place in which they were written), grammatical (the relationship of words to one another), etymological (word meaning), contextual setting (the relation of the text to the surrounding passage). If we read the Bible like this our lives will be transformed.

The Lord bless you as His truth enlightens your life and marriage. "Your word is a lamp to my feet and a light to my path" (Psalm 119:105).

Looking to God's Word, Exercise #1

Prayerfully, relying as you read on the illuminating ministry of God's Spirit, *humbly feast on Ephesians 5:21-33*. I would encourage you first to read through the entire epistle to the Ephesians three times. Divide the letter into two sections (chapters 1-3 and 4-6) and you will be able to do this in a six-day cycle.

Remember, in chapters 1-3 the apostle Paul lays down the great doctrinal foundation for Christian living (our position in Christ, our spiritual resources in the Lord, our unity in Jesus, etc.). Then chapters 4-6 flesh out that marvelous truth in practical living, including the gospel lived out and illustrated in our marriage relationship!

This simple step will give you a contextual understanding of the supreme passage in the Bible dealing with marriage (Ephesians 5:21-33). Read the text slowly, let it speak for itself, and make observations in a notebook as you go.

Secondly, make Ephesians 5:21-33 the focus of your devotional life for at least a week (in an exercise such as this more is better, e.g., two, or perhaps three weeks), reading through the passage once a day until your familiarity with the text grows. Feel free to use basic textual helps[1] as you have need, but spend the bulk of your time simply reading God's word prayerfully.

Lastly, I would encourage you to listen to some exceptional preaching on Ephesians 5:21-33. I would suggest Pastors John Piper, or John MacArthur as possible teachers for your enlightening odyssey through God's blueprint for your marriage. This part of the exercise will take you weeks, perhaps months as you carefully ingest God's health giving instruction. These faithful shepherds will guide you through the pastures of God's word with great care and insight, so enjoy the journey (Their resources are available through their respective ministries online: John Piper – Desiring God Ministries, www.desiringgod.org; John MacArthur – Grace To You, www.gty.org).

Again, allow the scripture to speak for itself, and make observations from the text in your study of God's principles for the marriage relationship. As these precepts become clear to you, and God's Spirit convicts your heart about how to strengthen your relationship, resolve to apply these truths to your marriage at the point of need.

Looking to God's Word, Exercise #2

Read Philippians 2:1-11 once per day for at least a week (again, more is better, use good Bible study tools as you have need).[2] Write down the biblical principles of humble living modeled by Christ in verses 1-11. Make a list of these principles on a notebook page numbering each of them.

As the text becomes clearer to you, ask yourself, *Are there any other passages in the Bible that highlight these principles?"* Check out the cross references in the margins of your Bible for each verse and read through them. Do these passages shed any light on the truth you have observed from Philippians 2:1-11? If so, write down your observations in your notebook by the appropriate principle.

As you think through the text daily and make your observations, review the precepts you have gleaned in the previous days. Don't hesitate to meditate and mull over the words of scripture and the truth you are learning.

Finally, begin a new page entitled "Action Steps" and consider "What practical actions can I take in my relationship to my spouse for each of the principles I have culled from Philippians 2:1-11 and other scriptures? What things can I do to put these biblical truths into action in my marriage?"

Obviously, you may start the "Action Steps" early in your study as obvious applications come to mind, but I would strongly encourage you to have a firm grip on what the text clearly teaches before you attempt extensive application. Once you properly understand the text you will be able to rightly apply it to your life and marriage.

Take your time doing this exercise. Approach Philippians 2:1-11 humbly knowing that it is God's word given to you for your welfare. Once again, consider the text carefully and allow it to say what it says without you reading a preconceived idea into it. If you spend the bulk of your time understanding the meaning of the text, discerning the biblical principles imbedded in the page, the practical applications to your particular context will become clear.

A Final Exhortation

I exhort you to follow the command of the great apostle Paul and "Let the word of Christ richly dwell within you" (Colossians 3:16). Interestingly, this reference (Colossians 3:16, verses 12-17 is the broader context)[3] is a parallel passage to Ephesians 5:15-21, the familiar text dealing with walking in the Spirit (which is also followed by God's blueprint for a godly marriage in v 21-33).[4]

We all desire to walk by the Spirit, to be changed by the Spirit, and according to Colossians 3:16 that personal transformation of God's Spirit begins and is sustained by allowing God's word ("the word of Christ") to fill our lives in an abundant manner. The Holy Spirit uses the truth of the word to bring about lasting change in our lives and in our relationships.

Indeed, walking by the Spirit is synonymous with walking in obedience to God's word through the power of the indwelling Spirit of God. May you be faithful to this essential Christian command, and may you experience the transformation God's Spirit will certainly bring.

If you approach these exercises with an earnest, hungry heart to know God's mind, this will prove to be a thrilling voyage of discovery that will impact your life and marriage profoundly. The Lord bless you as you seek to know Him and His desire for your life and marriage relationship.

Biblical Resources for Your Marriage

Money in Marriage (workbook with CD)
By: Larry Burkett & Michael E. Taylor

Lies Women Believe
By: Nancy Leigh DeMoss

Preparing for Marriage God's Way (premarital workbook)
By: Wayne Mack

Love That Lasts
By: Gary & Betsy Ricucci

Purity Principle
By: Randy Alcorn

Solving Marriage Problems
By: Jay E. Adams

Reforming Marriage
By: Douglas and Nancy Wilson

Excellent Wife
By: Martha Peace

Intimate Marriage (available from Ligonier Ministries, at www.ligonier.org)
By: R.C. Sproul

The Fulfilled Family – CD Series
By: John McArthur

Disciplines of a Godly Man
By: R. Kent Hughes

Disciplines of a Godly Woman
By: Barbara Hughes

When Sinners Say "I Do"
By: Dave Harvey

Strengthening Your Marriage
By: Wayne A. Mack

9marks.org
9Marks Marriage Book Comparison Chart
This is an excellent and trusted source to review over two dozen books on marriage for yourself.

CHAPTER THREE

The Undermining of the Parent/Child Relationship

The marriage relationship is one important arena where the enemy works his destructive desires, but it is not the only one. There is also an unprecedented and growing chorus of shrill and forceful voices screaming to undermine parental authority and "liberate" young people from the shackles of their domestic "oppression." In our increasingly secular way of life, this is the message parents and children continually hear. This message is part of the pervasive malignancy of our culture, cultivated and directed by the god of this world.

Since the fall of man, the devil has marked the pivotal relationship between parents and children for destruction. If he can undermine parental authority and wrench young people out from under the protection and direction of their parents, he will wreak destruction in their lives and bring devastation to the family.

A Pathetic Portrayal

On the one hand, parents are often portrayed today as clueless yet necessary benefactors. Within this false framework the main responsibility of parents in the child-rearing venture is to provide services and goods for an independent progeny. Perhaps even more disturbing is the contemporary rationale that parents have little authority and minimal credibility. Convention tells us this is normal, it is the way it is, and so we are counseled to wise up and get used to it. It is even pawned off on the masses with a positive spin.

In a recent commercial for adolescent drug and alcohol prevention, the following spiel was made to encourage parents to talk to their kids about drug abuse - especially if their kids were already dabbling in recreational drugs or drinking. The pitch stated in part, "As a parent it's hard to believe that your children would ever believe, or listen to a word you say." Says who? Since when? Thank you for that gem, Mr. Know-so-much!

You mean to tell me your kid is teetering on the precipice of a chemical addiction, his/her life hangs in the balance, and you *might* want to sheepishly broach the subject of the dangers of drug abuse with them - remembering all the while that your words mean little, and your authority is non existent? Is that supposed to empower parents and help kids?

This is how feebly parents are frequently characterized by our culture, "You might want to think about talking to your kids from time to time – especially if they're in trouble – but remember your words mean little to them because you have marginal credibility, and even less authority."

Premature Autonomy

On the flip side of this emasculated view of parenting, young people (who need the loving guidance of their father and mother) are pushed toward independence from their parents intellectually, emotionally, and practically. They may be largely, or completely dependent on their mom and dad for their daily needs and luxuries, but no matter, this is understood to be their entitlement, and – in a bizarre twist - so is their right to be free of their parents' leadership.

My friends, this is a ubiquitous message, and it is one of the most sinister affronts to the wellbeing of our families. If you emasculate parental authority, and lure young people into a premature autonomy, you are left with familial chaos and disintegration. By logical consequence, the conditions are created for a surrogate system (government, educational system, social programs, etc.) to step in, redefine, and control the restructured (dissolved) "family."

The eroding state of the parent/child relationship has been perpetrated in large measure by two widely held fallacies. The first false notion is what I call the myth of acceptable rebellion (especially in the teen years), and the other is the growing myth of powerless parents. Both are false and yet these axioms are widely accepted as common wisdom, if not inevitable reality in public parental dialogue.

The Myth of Tolerable Rebellion

Let's momentarily hone in on the subject of teen rebellion because there is so much confusion about this issue, even in contemporary Christian circles. If I had a dollar for every time I heard something like this from the mouth of parents, even Christian parents, I could actually afford to buy property in California. "Teen rebellion is normal. It is simply part of growing up, and therefore it is to be expected, tolerated, and accepted. They'll grow out of it." Have you heard that pandered before? Do you have friends or family members who believes this? Has this falsehood crept into your way of thinking? It is a pervasive message, isn't it, but is it true?

Obviously, there is the potential for young people to rebel. Sinful man will lean toward sinful behavior – rebellion – because it comes naturally, and there is certainly a confluence of factors in the teen years that may encourage some teens to defy authority. It is the acquiescence to the inevitability of such behavior I want to address. The question we must consider is, "Should Christian parents embrace the idea that teen rebellion is an acceptable part of adolescent development?" Many would tell us without hesitation this is so.

Allow me to let my referee's flag fly on this one and call an official time out. Let's stop and think about this. Where, may I ask, does the idea of justifiable rebellion originate? It certainly does not spring from scripture. Never, not ever, is "rebellion" viewed as tolerable, or acceptable in holy writ. In fact "rebellion" is the very sin that plunged the human race into perdition. How could we view such sin as acceptable?

Rebellion fueled by human pride is the terrible cause of every ill we suffer as creatures. Make a mental list of the worst sins you can imagine (child pornography, murder, the slaughter of the innocent, etc.), not only is rebellion at the core of each of these sins (rebellion against the Law of God, human conscience, and the laws of God-ordained government), but rebellion is the first cause of those sins because all this misery began for humanity when our first parents rebelled against our gracious Creator. Adam and Eve wanted to act, and indeed did act, independently of God. Rebellion proved to be absolutely ruinous to mankind.

This is why rebellion is always seen as altogether hideous in the Bible. Prideful rebellion is the face of the most repulsive, abominable enemy of God, the devil (Isaiah 14:12-20). How is it that we can tolerate the reflection of that visage in our own? Perhaps it is because we sometimes look to the world to define our assumptions and behavior rather than to scripture.

Our culture lauds rebellion as a kind of progressive virtue. In contemporary media and literature, rebellion is pawned off as a hip, attractive, 'James Dean-like' quality. Far from being understood as a negative characteristic, it is celebrated across our cultural-developmental spectrum. We often view rebellion as endearing, or "cute" in little children and admirable in our cultural icons.

However, if we look to God's word instead of our culture to define rebellion, we will come away with a very different picture of this age-old sin. The Bible always portrays an accurate image of what rebellion truly is. For example, in the book of Jude, the half brother of our Lord Jesus spared no words to sharply condemn the false teachers polluting the church with their error and licentiousness. Toward the end of his just diatribe, he sums up their condition with the worst indictment biblical testimony can muster against these treacherous teachers.

In Jude 11 he writes, "Woe to them (false teachers)! For they have gone the way of Cain (a rebellious, self styled worshiper and murderer), and for pay they have rushed headlong into the error of Balaam (a self-willed prophet for hire), *and perished in the rebellion of Korah*" (the chief self-promoting rebel who unjustly opposed Moses and Aaron; emphasis added). In other words, the sum, the core of the false teachers' sin was *rebellion* expressed in unrestrained self-indulgence and error.

Perhaps you are thinking to yourself, "Well Marcelo, Jude is addressing the terrible iniquities of hardened sinners against God. What we're talking about now is the simple rebellion of children, and not the miasmic debauchery of false teachers and willful prophets. Teen rebellion is not on the same par with that!"

I'm afraid the Bible does not parse rebellion quite that way. It speaks of all rebellion as extreme sin. This is exactly why the Old Testament Law prescribed the death penalty for grown rebellious children (Exodus 21:17; Leviticus 20:9; Deuteronomy 21:18-21). In the New Testament the apostle Paul categorizes the worst of sinners as "disobedient to parents" (those given over by God to their evil passions, Romans 1:30; as well as the shameless sinners of the "last days,"[1] 2 Timothy 3:2).

To the Lord, the sin of rebellion toward parents belongs in the extreme ledger of human high crimes committed against His holy character.

Perhaps the strongest language unveiling the seriousness of rebellion in any form is given to us by the prophet/priest Samuel on the day he confronted mutinous Saul with his insurrection against the Lord.

It fell to Saul to fulfill an age-old prophecy against the enemy of God and Israel, the Amalekites. The Lord had sworn early in Israel's history as a nation (during their exodus out of Egypt) that He would destroy the Amalekites for their unjustifiable hatred, opposition, and violence toward His people (Exodus 17:8-16; Numbers 24:30; 1 Samuel 15:2).

After nearly four hundred years, the time had come to execute God's judgment. Saul was in the unique position to accomplish the word of the Lord (1 Samuel 15:2, 3). Imagine being in a place where you could literally fulfill a biblical prophecy. What a privilege! Instead, Saul chose to fulfill his own selfish, political agenda (1 Samuel 15:7-9). In Saul's eyes his deviation from God's command was likely nothing more than savvy pragmatism (1 Samuel 15:13-15), but in truth was insurrection against God, rebellion.

In 1 Samuel 15:22, 23 we read the familiar but sobering words of Samuel the man of God, "Has the LORD as much delight in burnt offerings and sacrifices as in obeying the voice of the LORD? Behold, to obey is better than sacrifice, and to heed than the fat of rams. For rebellion is as the sin of divination, and insubordination is as iniquity and idolatry. Because you have rejected the word of the LORD, He has also rejected you from being king."

God through Samuel tells us that rebellion in any form is tantamount to the practice of the occult, or witchcraft and equal - in God's mind

- to the futility of pagan idolatry. What's more, unrepentant rebellion will lead to serious discipline from the Lord as it did in Saul's life. Rebellion is no small issue to God.

You may call "rebellion" in children a lot of things biblically, but you can never call it tolerable, or acceptable, or "cute" anymore than you can call the practice of witchcraft and idol worship reasonable and justifiable. For you and I to tolerate rebellion in our offspring is to openly invite God's opposition against ourselves and our progeny. Is that tolerable? Never!

The Myth of Powerless Parents

A second false precept of parenting that has virtually become an unquestioned maxim in this day and age is the myth of powerless parents. Many parents feel powerless to lead and exercise loving supervision over their children, particularly their older children. They have bought into the flimsy notion that when children enter their preteen and teen years parents must - by default - relinquish much of their authority to their young people and/or youth experts who possess more teen savvy and youthful credibility (e.g., assorted mentors such as educators, sports coaches, and frequently even youth pastors). The incessant, and increasingly loud message parents hear is that they have precious little say in shepherding their young people.

Quite honestly this monotonous drivel is a myth peddled by secular culture. It has no foundation in God's word, and sadly, many Christian parents unwittingly embrace this error to some degree. In regard to Christians, I don't believe this is a high-handed sin of parental abdication for most believers; however, it is inadvertently accepted as the status quo dogma for the teen years.

Though not often admitted in a public forum (secular or Christian), the practical consensus is parents should stick to being human vending machines in order to pony up a cornucopia of goods and services. They should provide shuttle services to desired activities, supply housing, and function as the financiers of the education of choice, etc. Moreover, parents must see to it that they supply commodities as well. This would include, but not be limited to, functioning as living/breathing 24/7 cash machines, purveyors of the latest clothing fads and techno-goods (cell phones, X-Boxes, iPods, ad infinitum).

In other words, according to today's expectations, parents are tolerated because they are around to provide a certain lifestyle for their children with unbroken consistency - and of course without meddling in the young people's affairs. To sum up, parents are like piggy banks: a good source of revenue but powerless to influence those who empty them. When it comes to children, parents are duty bound to provide, but have little actual authority to lead.

Furthermore, the world would have us believe parents have no authority to guide their children in relationships and courtship, or to determine reasonable bounds of modesty. Popular opinion would suggest that parental powers should not regulate "rights" such as cell phones, use of vehicles, computers, etc. And certainly some would argue that mom and dad have no business "hanging out" with their children especially if their friends, or youth mentors are around, etc., etc, etc. I believe there is a theological term for such thinking, bologna!

CHAPTER FOUR

The Biblical Pattern of Domestic Leadership & Submission

These two falsehoods, the myth of acceptable teen rebellion and the "Powerless Parent" myth, are what the world vomits at our feet and expects us to accept as tried and true wisdom. Tragically as I said, many Christians buy into aspects of this futile way of thinking. However, let me say this as clearly as I can, such nonsense (like the acceptability of rebellion) has absolutely no biblical basis and is in fact the antithesis of what God prescribes for families in His clear word.

God designed the institution of the home to run under the authority of the parents. This is true both for believers and unbelievers, but Christian parents must understand that they are bound by biblical imperative to lead their children in God's ways into young adulthood (Genesis 18:19; Deuteronomy 6:7; 11:19; Psalm 78:4; Proverbs 22:6; Ephesians 6:4; 2 Timothy 1:5; 3:15), and children in a believing home must embrace submission to parents. They must view their parents biblically, as their God-given shepherds, protectors, and providers for early life. This is the Lord's demand of them for their good (Exodus 20:12; Deuteronomy 5:16; Proverbs 6:20; 23:22; Matthew 15:3-9; Ephesians 6:1; Ephesians 6:2, 3; Colossians 3:20).

The fable is parents are powerless to lead their growing children, and young people need to be free of their parents' control. The truth is parents have the biblical and moral authority to shepherd their children, and children are blessed to submit to them. This is God's pattern for our families, and aligning our lives with this plan will result in great blessing.

Augustine echoed this very message when he wrote, "The peace of a home lies in the ordered harmony of authority and obedience between the members of a family living together." Reciprocation between these two biblical principles (authority and obedience) leads to peace in the home.

My dear fellow parents, you have the biblical privilege, and noble duty to lovingly and sacrificially lead your maturing flock at home. You are not powerless or helpless to lead the souls God has entrusted to you. Children, remember God has not left you without shepherds to protect, guide and to provide for you.

I challenge you to look to the scripture to define your roles in the home. I exhort you to let God set the pattern for your family and not pop culture. With that in mind, let's briefly consider some biblical examples that model God's blueprint for the home (i.e., parental leadership and the submission of children to parents).

Simple observation into the culture of the Bible teaches us children remained under the authority of their parents until their late teens and into early adulthood. In large measure their sojourn under their parents' care continued until marriage – much as it has in our recent cultural past.

Through the years of metamorphosis from childhood to young adulthood, godly parents shepherded their familial flock in the fear of the Lord[1] The Bible testifies that young people, for their part, subjected themselves to the authority of their parents' leadership. It is also clear that progeny exercised great deference to parents even when independent from them - let alone when living with them.

In the biblical paradigm, while the roles and relationship between parents and children develop and mature over time,[2] the clear biblical pattern of parental authority and submission of children is the repeated theme and model.

The Example of Job and His Children

Take for example the model of Job's family. The spiritual oversight Job employed over his children and their great respect for their father stands out in startling contrast to the parent/child relationship we see espoused today. The background narrative (chapters 1 and 2) preceding the principle thrust of the book (chapters 3-42) offers some basic information about Job, the man, and in the process unfolds some key insights into the relationship he had with his sons and daughters.

First, we learn Job was a godly man who had a quiver full of kids. We read in Job 1:1, 2, "There was a man in the land of Uz whose name was Job; and that man was blameless, upright, fearing God and turning away from evil. Seven sons and three daughters were born to him." In this short introductory narrative (Job 1:1-5) we pick up Job's story well into his parenting venture. Verse four tells us, "His sons used to go and hold a feast in the house of each one on his day, and they would send and invite their three sisters to eat and drink with them."

This tells us that it is plausible, if not apparent, that Job's seven sons and three daughters were grown and on their own. The respective spouses and children were likely omitted from the record for the sake of economy of words so as to get to the central theme of the book, the testing and persevering trust of godly Job. That there is an amazing economy of words is blatantly obvious because we are not given the names of any of Job's children even though they were exceedingly precious to him, as we shall see.[3]

What is certain is that each son had his own "house" where all the siblings (and no doubt extended family if there was any) would dine together for the chief meal of the day in a seven-day rotation. Obviously, this was a family that relished being together. It seems clear that the sons at least, were old enough to live on their own, and independent enough to host a weekly family get together. The simple point here is Job's children, particularly his sons and likely his daughters, were grown adults.

In light of this context, the leadership Job exercised toward his sons and daughters in verse five is truly amazing. They were grown and on their own, and yet Job led them as a priest to worship the God they served. What is equally refreshing is Job's children willingly submitted and followed their father's spiritual leadership. Listen to the words of verse five.

"When the days of feasting had completed their cycle, Job would send and consecrate them, rising up early in the morning and offering burnt offerings according to the number of them all; for Job said, 'Perhaps my sons[4] have sinned and cursed God in their hearts.' Thus Job did continually."

After a week of daily celebrations as a family clan, on the eighth day Job would "send" or call his family out from their normal routines and "consecrate them" for the appointed purpose of worshipping God. The term "consecrate" (in verse 5) can also be translated "holy"[5] and carries the idea of "setting apart"[6] for God. In other words, Job would summon His children from their day-to-day activities and prepare them spiritually to worship. The evident response is Job's family gathered under their father's guidance to bow their hearts before their Creator and gracious Benefactor.

Let me make two simple observations from this plain narrative. The first is this: Job led his family spiritually. The second reality is his children followed. True, this observation may not be rocket science, but it forms the simple yet strong foundation of familial health and peace.

The priority of parents is to occupy themselves with the diligent, loving, spiritual leadership of their children without becoming detached, reactionary providers. This is what children need most from parents, and it is the joyful obligation of children to submit to their parent's spiritual guidance.

Notice also that Job's spiritual leadership is a practice given to us without time parameters. The text says, "Thus Job did continually." This suggests a long-standing habit of spiritual leadership and deference that reached far back into their family history, from the earliest days and into early adulthood.

Learning from the Life of David

This same pattern of parental authority and respect/obedience in young people is readily seen in the early life of David, the shepherd who would be king. In 1 Samuel 16:11 we're introduced to David as the "youngest" of Jesse's sons whose job it was to tend the family's sheep.

David was no doubt in his late teens at this time for he may have been too young to fight for Israel's army, and yet a little later in this same passage he is described as "a skillful musician, a mighty man of valor, a warrior, one prudent in speech, and a handsome man; and the LORD is with him" (1 Samuel 16:18).

Also the Hebrew term *na'ar* is used to describe David in 1 Samuel 17:42. The word is largely dependent on its context for meaning and is employed in the Old Testament to refer to a young man in his late teens or early manhood.[7] That meaning fits the context of 1 Samuel 16-17 best. David was not quite an adult male of military age, yet he had the physical strength and emotional bravery to chase down a bear and a lion, seize them by their beards and kill them to save sheep (1 Samuel 17:34-36).

That, my friends, is what I would call "jutzpah," nerve! No child would dare attempt such a rescue, but a young man in his physical prime with the emotional certitude of youth and ironclad faith in God might have the audacity to take on wild beasts and kill them. As for me, even in my youthful prime, I would have used a gun! No gun? Let the beasts have the sheep! Clearly, David was at the peak of his youthful vigor.

So David was likely a physically mature teenager whose responsibilities suited his age – tending his father's flock. What is interesting in this exciting and familiar account of 1 Samuel 16-17 is even though David was unbelievably strong, gifted and intelligent, he was also humble and continued in subjection to his father.

While his older brothers Eliab, Abinadab, and Shammah were off fighting the Philistines (pretty heady and exciting stuff!), David in subjection to his father's wishes was at home keeping company with sheep – not the smartest, nor the most interesting creatures on earth. (My apologies to any Basque sheepherders reading this book.) Yet there is never a clue in the text of dissatisfaction in David, nor the slightest hint of insubordination. David did not have an inflated view of his own importance and willingly submitted himself to his father, Jesse. That's a humble, obedient, contented young guy, and that's the type of young man God loves to use. David was ready to begin his climb to greatness and his assent began with a simple and sincere act of dutiful obedience to his father.

Desiring to receive news of his sons on the battlefront, Jesse sent David with provisions for his brothers and also to bring back a report of their condition. In 1 Samuel 17:17-20, Jesse dispatched his son on a simple errand, which the Lord used to catapult young David into the national limelight and into the hearts of the people of Israel. Notably, it all began with a food run and a young man's willingness to submit to his aged father.

"Then Jesse said to David his son, 'Take now for your brothers an ephah of this roasted grain and these ten loaves and run to the camp to your brothers. Bring also these ten cuts of cheese to the commander of their thousand, and look into the welfare of your brothers, and bring back news of them. For Saul and they and all the men of Israel are in the valley of Elah, fighting with the Philistines.' (Now notice this first sentence in verse 20.) "So David arose early in the morning and left the flock with a keeper and took the supplies and went as Jesse had commanded him."

I love the simplicity of that narrative! Even though David could have complained that he was worthy of fighting alongside his brothers, certainly he was at least their equal or better in strength and valor, he humbly stayed with the sheep because he was obedient to his father's wishes. He didn't complain, he didn't take out his frustration on the sheep, he didn't disobey and circumvent his father's wishes, he simply submitted himself to the authority God had placed in his life – a far cry from how his future son Absalom would respond to David!

Later when his father directed his steps away from the herd to serve his brothers on the field, David arranged for the care of the sheep, and simply complied with his father's directive. "So David arose early in the morning … took the supplies and went as Jesse had commanded him." As they say, 'the rest is history,' isn't it? David found enormous blessing through habitual and simple obedience. Jesse led his son,

David submitted to his father, and God's favor flowed to this faithful son, humble shepherd, King of Israel, and lover of God.

"He also chose David His servant and took him from the sheepfolds; from the care of the ewes with suckling lambs He brought him to shepherd Jacob His people, and Israel His inheritance. So he shepherded them according to the integrity of his heart, and guided them with his skillful hands" (Psalm 78:70-72).

The pattern found in the first chapter of the book of Job and in the life of David is understood (accepted) throughout the Old Testament. Children remained under the authority of their parents into young adulthood. The parents for their part exercised guardianship over their progeny, and when the children flew from the family nest to establish their own homes, there was still a sincere deference for parents. God's clear design is for parents to lead their children and for children to respect their parents, and it is faithful adherence to God's blueprint that results in the Lord's benediction.

The plain and unmistakable point is that parents have biblical authority to lead. They are not helpless. They have the right to lead their children (even teens), and children (including teens) are in a place of blessing when they submit to and follow the leadership of their father and mother. This is God's design for the Christian home.

The Template Left by the Lord Jesus

One stunning biblical example of godly, adolescent submission to parental authority is found in the New Testament. The reason this example stands out is because it is the pattern of the Lord Jesus Himself. Jesus, God in the flesh, willingly submitted Himself to His earthly parents whom He had created, for whom He would die an atoning death, and over whom He would rule as their resurrected, sovereign Master.

God Almighty as a human boy progressed into early adulthood and blossomed in wisdom (Luke 2:52). Increasingly as the young Lord Jesus matured, the glory of His Father, the splendor of His kingdom, and the magnitude of His redemptive task grew ever greater in His mind and heart. Although His parents understood something of the uniqueness of their Son (Matthew 1:18-24; Luke 1:26-38; 46-55; 2:19, 51), they could not fully enter into the vision for the mission the Father progressively revealed to the Son through the scripture by His Spirit.

In fact, as time diminished the clarity of those early days in Nazareth and Bethlehem, Joseph and Mary failed to adequately apprehend their Son's growing, righteous appetites. Jesus as an adolescent could rightly say, "My parents don't understand my heart of hearts." The gap in knowledge and awareness between He and His parents became distressingly clear one particular spring in the bud of our Lord's adolescence.

When Jesus was 12 years old His parents took Him to Jerusalem. In the year of His thirteenth birthday and Bar Mitzvah, like most observant Jewish boys, Jesus was taken to Jerusalem to participate in the Passover feast. There the sights and sounds of the Holy City and the great feast surrounded him. His heart must have welled up with a mixture of excitement, reverence, and destiny. He was in the Holy City; He walked among the throng of the congregation of Israel; He heard the priest sound the shofar in the temple courts, and at last He worshipped in His Father's house. This is where He needed to be. He felt at home in the temple of God.

Luke 2:46 introduces us to the Lord Jesus at the temple. It is interesting to note that we find the promised Messiah (Isaiah 9:6, 7; Luke 1:31-33), the Agent of creation (Colossian 1:16), the Son of God (John 20:31), the high King of heaven (Revelation 19:16) deferentially reciprocating with the teachers of Israel.

We read that Jesus was "sitting in the midst of the teachers, both listening to them and asking them questions," and even though "all who heard Him were amazed at His understanding and His answers" (Luke 2:47), His interaction was undergirded by humility and respect toward the adults of His youth.

But again, the young Messiah was at home in the temple of the living God. How He must have relished this rite of passage in the heart of Zion. Truly, there was no other place on earth where He longed to be more than in the temple of the God of Israel.

After the momentous celebration, Mary and Joseph packed up their belongings and began their trek home in the exuberant cavalcade of relatives and friends. No doubt joyful over the great feast and at leisure in the ease of familiar faces, they started their sixty plus mile trip home assuming Jesus was in the caravan of relatives. A day into their journey they discovered to their troubled surprise that Jesus was not anywhere in the convoy.

Desperate to find their Son, they returned to Jerusalem where they searched for Him for three days. They looked for Jesus high and low, here, there and everywhere except in the most logical place of all, the temple. Luke 2:46 says, "Then, after three days they found Him in the temple, sitting in the midst of the teachers, both listening to them and asking them questions."

Why did it take them three days to find their Son? It took them a painfully long time because Joseph and Mary did not fully understand their Son's heart, nor did they accurately perceive God's plan for Him. Their lack of understanding led to misplaced indignation.

In Luke 2:48 we read, "When they saw Him (when they finally found Jesus in the temple) they were astonished.[8] The Lord's parents were emotionally overwhelmed, frantic at the temporary loss of their Son, and apparently these emotions erupted in a flush of shocked surprise when they at last found Him sitting among the sages of Jerusalem. Apparently, Joseph and Mary attributed the intense fear and distress they had experienced to the young Lord Jesus, and so His mother said to Him, "Son, *why have You treated us this way?* Behold, Your father and I have been anxiously looking for You."[9]

Our Lord's answer to His parents revealed their inability to grasp the uniqueness of His person and mission, and the logical place this comprehension would have taken their search. "And He said to them, 'Why is it that you were looking for Me? Did you not know that I had to be in My Father's house?' But they did not understand the statement which He had made to them" (Luke 2:49, 50).

Contemplation of what Joseph and Mary factually knew about their Son (i.e., what had been revealed to them thirteen years earlier), combined with what they perceived daily in their Son's life - perfect obedience, an obvious passion for the God of Israel and His House (John 2:13-17; Mark 11:15-18), certainly a great love and grasp of God's Law (Luke 2:47), should have lead them to the temple first. The plain fact is the Lord's parents were clearly out of step with their Son's heart, which was perfectly in tune with the Father's priorities.

If anyone had the right to lay aside the yoke of parental authority it would have been the Lord Jesus. He was after all the Son of God. His earthly parents did not understand - as clearly as He - heaven's prerogatives. They could not comprehend His burning desire to be about His Father's business. There was no way they could grasp the basic truths of His atoning work that was becoming increasingly clear to the maturing Son of Man.

And yet our Lord at this particular stage of life, and in the adolescent years that followed, willingly submitted Himself to the authority of His earthly parents. Knowing the human imperfections of His mother and father, and the sinless deity of the Lord Jesus Christ, Luke 2:51 is truly remarkable and powerfully instructive. Following the incident at the temple we read these astonishing words, "And He went down with them and came to Nazareth, and He continued in subjection to them."

The Lord Jesus submitted Himself to His parents not because they were better capable of directing His life than He was, but because this was God's pattern for the family. Furthermore, it was right for Joseph and Mary to lead their Son, and it was obedience to God's word that compelled our Lord to follow their leadership in His early years.

Not only does this example give us a pattern to follow, it clearly shows us the high regard the Father and the Son have for the familial structure God has ordained. Parents are not powerless providers, nor are children an authority unto themselves. Parents have a divine mandate to shepherd their children, and children have the privilege to submit to their parents. Herein is God's provision for their protection and wellbeing. It is this interchange of authority and obedience that will know the favorable smile of God.

It is no wonder the enemy panders the blather that parents are powerless and children autonomous. He wants to throw God's institution into chaos and rob us of God's great blessing.

Leadership and Obedience, the Path to Peace and Order in the Home

Many Christian families are in chaos, and indeed, at war because they fail to conform their homes to the principles of parental leadership and childhood submission. Without the active presence of these basic and guiding principles the family will pull itself apart with strife.

Describing the collaboration between authority and obedience in the family, St. Augustine penned, "From this care (reference to 1 Timothy 5:8) arises that peace of the home which lies in the harmonious interplay of authority and obedience among those who live there. For, those who have the care of the others give the orders (i.e., lead) – a man to his wife, parents to their children, masters to their servants. And those who are cared for must obey – wives their husbands, children their parents, servants their masters."[10]

Augustine's point is simple: peace in the home is the result of exercised authority and willful submission. Without this "harmonious interplay" the opposite of peace reigns, i.e., strife, animosity, disrespect, rebellion, etc. Authority and submission are the rails on which the blessed family runs, and authority constitutes the logical priority in this equation, for without it what would we obey?

Believing husbands and parents must employ their God given charge, and children in turn supply obedience. But please notice the noble kind of authority God calls believing parents to exercise. Augustine continues,

"In the home of a religious man (i.e., a true Christian) … those who command serve those whom they appear to rule – because, of course, they do not command out of lust to domineer, but out of a sense of duty – not out of pride like princes but out of solicitude like parents."[11] This is the kind of biblical authority Christ expects from Christian parents, and this is the kind of leadership our families desperately need.

CHAPTER FIVE

Authority Verses Authoritarianism

So far we've looked at two major fronts on which the world assaults the family: the marriage union and the parent/child relationship. We have just stressed the importance of the interplay between parental leadership and submission (of children) in the home. Before we consider one last battlefront in the war for the family, I want to pick up on the closing thought of the great St. Augustine in chapter four.

Allow me to give a brief and important word of caution about confusing biblical authority with "authoritarianism." There is a vast difference between controlling our children to appease ourselves (a type of authoritarianism), and lovingly, sacrificially leading them with their best interest in view (biblical leadership).

Authoritarianism is a term we usually associate with oppressive, heavy handed, totalitarian regimes. Whether speaking of a government or a person, we use it to describe the kind of rule that demands blind obedience from the rank and file, with little concern for their welfare. The motivation of such governance revolves around selfish ambition secured by unflinching control.

Leading Jesus' Way

Sadly, leaders of this ilk - in government and in every facet of leadership - have been the rule rather than the exception throughout human history. The Lord Jesus made reference to this reality in Matthew 20:25. In the final days of the Lord's pre-resurrection ministry, the disciples began to jockey for position as they anticipated the coming millennial kingdom. The cross was not yet a part of their soteriological and eschatological scheme.[1] They truly believed the next step in God's redemptive plan was the establishment of the kingdom promised to David (Luke 19:11).

They lacked understanding of the Lord's mission. They could not yet wrap their minds around the death and resurrection of Christ, nor the kingdom values He espoused in His Sermon On The Mount (Matthew 5-7:29). At this juncture of their lives and ministry, they selfishly defined the Lord's reign in terms of their own self-interests.

Regrettably, their pride sprouted and flourished as a noxious weed and drove them to dominate one another. Seeing this, Jesus spoke a word of correction to His disciples, "But Jesus called them to Himself and said, 'You know that the rulers of the Gentiles lord it over them, and their great men exercise authority over them.'"

With that statement, Jesus spoke directly to the sinful struggle of the twelve. The thrust of the entire sentence is summarized in the Greek verb "lord" (katakurieuo). The term carries the idea of forceful control of another and could be translated "to overpower" or "to subdue."[2] The primary word means "to rule," but it is compounded by a preposition that "conveys the sense of rule to one's own advantage".[3] Furthermore, the grammar of the verb (present, active, indicative) also communicates a continuous mode of behavior. In other words, Jesus tells us that the modus operandi of ungodly leadership continually seeks to subdue people for selfish ends.

That this is a danger within the Christian community is clear from the direct warning the Lord issued to His men. Drawing a contrast to the world, Jesus said, "It is not this way among you." The word "not" is in the emphatic position, the first word of the verse, so that the Greek literally reads "NOT in this way is it with you." We're not to exercise authority as the world does. Our "way" of leading, Christ's "way" of authority stands out in blazing contrast to the domineering, self-serving ways of men. So, how do disciples of Christ exercise authority?

The answer follows in the balance of verse 26 and in verse 27. Jesus instructed His men with these words, "but whoever wishes to become great among you shall be your servant, and whoever wishes to be first among you shall be your slave." The way to lead and exercise authority among the people of God is through humble, sacrificial service. This is the way of Christ, and just to make sure the disciples and their spiritual progeny (you and I) got the message, Jesus put forth the example of His very life and mission in verse 28, "just as the Son of Man did not come to be served, but to serve, and to give His life a ransom for many."

Lamentably, even after this correction, the Lord's disciples still did not get the message. In fact, they continued their maneuvering and posturing for more than a week clear into the night of the Lord's betrayal. They were not walking in the way of Christ. They were mimicking the world's style of self-promotion for self gain.

Blinded by their own pride they could not see the pathetic unseemliness of their behavior. Then the Lord, in love and with great patience, showed them His way once more. Gathering for their last Passover together, the Master gave His men an object lesson that would expose their bloated egos, and ultimately alter their understanding of biblical leadership. In John 13:1-5 we read,

> "Now before the Feast of the Passover, Jesus knowing that His hour had come that He would depart out of this world to the Father, having loved His own who were in the world,

He loved them to the end. During supper, the devil having already put into the heart of Judas Iscariot, the son of Simon, to betray Him, Jesus, knowing that the Father had given all things into His hands, and that He had come forth from God and was going back to God, *got up⁴ from supper, and *laid aside His garments; and taking a towel, He girded Himself. Then He *poured water into the basin, and began to wash the disciples' feet and to wipe them with the towel with which He was girded."

The great King, the Son of God led His men by modeling humble service. Soon after this gracious act, Jesus Christ willingly laid down His life to save the ones He loved, thus giving His people the supreme example of sacrificial leadership. That's the model of leadership we need to follow in the church, and certainly also in the Christian home.

Biblical authority to lead the home means parents have the joy and privilege of serving their children with biblically informed, humble, loving leadership, motivated by God's glory and their children's best interests.

Too often I have witnessed children and young people crushed by parents who control them with an iron fist largely to gratify their personal (the parents') selfish interests. Some of these folks have a compulsive desire to control and domineer. Others struggle with impatience and quash childish play and curiosity with a myriad of unnecessary corrections to satisfy their own warped sense of order.

Some exercise authority from the mixed well of anxiety. Worried to the point of paranoia that their children might be polluted by the world, they substitute loving authority for rigid legalism and in the process rob their children of joy and deprive themselves of their children's friendship. Still others live vicariously through their offspring and push them to achieve (sports, academia, etc.) in order to feed their own pride.

Regardless of how despotic authority expresses itself, at its core it dominates for its own gratification. That is the world's way, and if we parent by those guidelines, we will likely experience the world's results - fractured families and devastated lives.

Our parental leadership/authority must mirror that of the Lord Jesus. You may ask, "Synthesized to its essence, what does this look like? What are the distinguishing marks of Christ-like parental leadership?" Without being exhaustive, keep in mind four evident principles that arise out of the two texts we considered in the previous paragraphs (Matthew 20:24-28; John 13:1-5).

The Marks of Godly Leadership

Godly parenting, like godly leadership of any kind, is marked by:

1) Unconditional love, "...having loved His own who were in the world, He loved them to the end" (i.e., with a "perfect love"[5]). The Lord Jesus loves us with a perfect love. His love is always patient, kind and never failing, etc. (1 Corinthians 13). While we cannot love perfectly at all times, we can exercise that same type of virtue, otherwise we would not have the exhortation in scripture to pursue it. It is Christ-like love children must experience from their parents.

If children know their parents love them with a God-given love that seeks their continual welfare, transcends performance, corrects sinful behavior, perseveres in forgiveness, and delights in them as objects of affection, they will have a context in which to grow into spiritual health. Few things will engender respect, obedience, and affection in children more than the kind of unconditional love we experience in our Lord Jesus.

Fervent Christ-like love will also overcome many of our faults and failures as parents. The apostle Peter in his exhortation to the church reminds us of an important guiding principle for all relationships including the one parents enjoy with their children. The scripture reminds us, "Above all, keep fervent in your love for one another, because love covers a multitude of sins" (1 Peter 4:8).[6]

2) Additionally, biblical parenting expresses itself *in godly example,* "Jesus ... *got up[7] from supper, and *laid aside His garments; and taking a towel, He girded Himself." (John 13:4, see also verses 14, 15). Having taught His disciples what true leadership was, Jesus fleshed out these very principles by example for the disciples to see and follow.

Like Jesus, biblical leadership models the truth it preaches. Parents cannot lead their children where they are unwilling to go, nor can they hope their sons and daughters will follow a "theoretical lifestyle" they see compromised on the stage of life. The old copout, "Do as I say, not as I do" will erode our credibility, emasculate our authority, and ultimately lead future generations down a ruinous road. Parents must lead by example.

3) Christ-like parental leadership is also characterized by *humble, sacrificial service,* "Then He *poured water into the basin, and began to wash the disciples' feet and to wipe them with the towel with which He was girded" (John 13:5). Of course this humble act of service by our Lord Jesus was but a flicker of the sacrificial flame that would burn brightly on Calvary's cross. Soon the disciples would behold the single greatest act of humble service ever rendered for the good of man.

That unique sacrifice saved us, but the cross, along with the selfless life that culminated there, left an example for us to follow. This is Paul's main point in describing the self-emptying of the Lord Jesus,

"Do nothing from selfishness or empty conceit, but with humility of mind regard one another as more important than yourselves; do not merely look out for your own personal interests, but also for the interests of others. Have this attitude in yourselves which was also in Christ Jesus, who, although He existed in the form of God, did not regard equality with God a thing to be grasped, but emptied Himself, taking the form of a bond-servant, and being made in the likeness of men. Being found in appearance as a man, He humbled Himself by becoming obedient to the point of death, even death on a cross" (Philippians 2:3-8).

Like the example epitomized in Jesus Christ, *Christian* leadership is *sacrificial* leadership.

From time to time I hear Christian parents express their perceived "right" to "personal time" and expenditures away from their kids (day spa, shopping with friends, golf, etc.) with almost religious fervor. Certainly we all need refreshment, and husbands and wives would do well to spell each other from the stresses of life and child rearing as needs arise.

However, we must remember Christian parenting, like Christian leadership in other areas (e.g., ministry, marriage, etc.), is a call to lose ourselves in the service of another. Often we will have to lay aside personal desires, prerogatives, and even needs (perceived or real) to assure our children receive the care and guidance they require. This is the manner in which Christ served us, and it is the way we must lead our families.

4) Finally, Christian parenting is *motivated by the wellbeing of those under our care,* "just as the Son of Man did not come to be served, but to serve, and to give His life a ransom for many" (Matthew 20:28). Why did Jesus take on the horror of the cross and on it suffer the infinite wrath of God against our sin? It was because there was no other way to bring about our eternal wellbeing in salvation (Matthew 26:39; John 13:1). He took upon Himself the full burden of our sins so that we might receive the full benefit of His righteousness (2 Corinthians 5:21). Jesus, the good shepherd, was driven to the cross for our wellbeing.

Likewise, the way of our Master directs us to shepherd our children with their good clearly in focus. To be sure this means that we make prudent decisions for their earthly prosperity (health, education, etc.), but it also means that we guide them with the welfare of their souls as our main objective. One of my favorite promoted pastors (he's graduated to the presence of the Chief Shepherd) wrote about this very issue more than a century ago. Wisely he observed,

"This is the thought that should be uppermost on your mind in all you do for your children (*the wellbeing of our children's souls*). In every step you take about them, in every plan, and scheme, and arrangement that concerns them, do not leave out that mighty question, "How will this affect their souls?"

"Soul love is the soul of all love. To pet and pamper and indulge your child, as if this world was all he had to look to, and this life the only season for happiness - to do this is not true love, but cruelty. It is treating him like some beast of the earth, which has but one world to look to, and nothing after death. It is hiding from him that grand truth, which he ought to be made to learn from his very infancy, that the chief end of his life is the salvation of his soul."[8] To be faithful to this primary objective is to shepherd our children with their true welfare in mind.

Do these virtues describe the general thrust of your parental leadership? It is true that children must obey their parents, but Christian parents are obliged to exercise the kind of humble leadership Jesus exemplified. Without selfless leadership, deferential obedience is often replaced with mechanical obligation at best, willful rebellion at worst and disaster riding in the wake of dissension.

A FEW WORDS OF APPLICATION FOR THE CHRISTIAN HOME

PART ONE

Two Important Principles to Strengthen Your Family

As I write this book I am the happy husband of my bride of twenty-five years (Valorie) and the proud father of four amazing, loving children (two college students, Josh 22, Rebekah 18; one high schooler, Josiah 16; and a middle schooler, Aaron 11). Bar none, these have been the happiest years of my life, but they haven't been without their share of hurdles, potholes, and an occasional careening off the side of the road – largely due to my own driving!

Through the years I have made more than my allowances of mistakes as a husband and father. There are things I did and said that I wish I hadn't. There are things I didn't do, or say that I would today given the opportunity. There were undertakings I felt were more important than they actually were, and other tasks that deserved more attention than I was willing to give them. Unfortunately, unlike my computer, life does not come with a "reset" button I can push when my activity causes life to "freeze up" or "crash." Like kids on a playground I think we all wish we could call "Do over!" when the outcome of our decisions are less than stellar.

Nevertheless, there are two pursuits I do not regret emphasizing in our home. In the midst of our imperfect journey they have proved to be fruitful priorities for my family and myself. Allow me to simply mention them and put them forward for your prayerful consideration.

First of all, I encourage you to commit yourself to the priority of a relationship with Jesus Christ personally, and in the life of your family. Secondly, determine to spend more time with your spouse and children. These two commitments are not difficult to understand, but they can be a challenge to fulfill. The world and its priorities continually attempt to pull us away from these strength-giving pursuits.

Committing Ourselves to Fellowship with the Lord Jesus

God's pattern for the family involves a mingling of loving leadership exercised by the parents, and complimented by the humble submission of children. For the Christian family both these virtues (love and humility), and duties (leadership and submission) are the outgrowth of the believer's relationship to Jesus Christ.

In Him we learn the nature of true love (John 15:9, 12, 13; Ephesians 5:2), humility (Matthew 11:29; Philippians 2:8), leadership (Matthew 4:19; 9:9; 16:24; John 10:4, 27; 21:22), and submission (Luke 22:42; John 4:34; 5:30; 6:38).

If we hope to nurture these same characteristics in our families, we must understand that this hope centers on the person of Jesus Christ and our relationship to Him. *Christ*ian virtue is rooted in, and springs forth from *Christ*. It takes root in our heart and blossoms in our lives because we are in Him and therefore becoming more like Him. Without a vital, vibrant relationship to Jesus Christ, Christian virtue easily degrades into moral duty, and moral duty by itself (without the sustaining love and fellowship of Christ) will fail to transform us.

Therefore the greatest exhortation I can give to myself, my wife, my sons and daughter, and truly, to all Christian parents and children is this, *make it your greatest ambition to love the Lord Jesus Christ.* Call out to Him with an earnest heart. Seek Him diligently through the pages of the Bible. Talk to Him through the glad venue of prayer, and ask God to conform your life to His. Quite honestly, that is our only hope for true reform, both for our lives and for our families.

This week I received correspondence from a mother who desired to throw in the towel on life. She professed to be a Christian, yet loathed her life as a wife and mother. She was sick of the cleaning and assorted domestic drudgeries, obviously unhappy with her marriage, and deeply disgruntled with her children. Tired of it all she confessed she was seriously contemplating abandoning her family. They simply were not making her happy!

There were many problems with this woman's letter, her approach, her focus, but the key element that was sadly missing from her words was the lack of any reference to Jesus Christ; to His pastoral care in her life, to His real, internal presence in the midst of her wrestling with depression and confusion. There was no allusion to her love for Him, nor His measureless love for her, her family. This poor woman was alone with her anger, and her silent rage crowded out the fellowship of Jesus Christ.

My dear brothers and sisters the only way to experience incremental and lasting transformation in our lives and families is through a growing relationship with the Lord Jesus. If our relationship to Him is not an organic one, then eventually we simply implode under the weight of our own misery. But if we continue to behold Him -

i.e., as we come to know Him through the truth of His word – the beauty of His character (His glory) and the power of His Spirit will progressively conform us to His image.

The great apostle Paul put it this way in 2 Corinthians 3:18, "But we all, with unveiled face, beholding as in a mirror the glory of the Lord, are being transformed into the same image from glory to glory, just as from the Lord, the Spirit." I invite you as a fellow Christian pilgrim and parent to make your relationship with Jesus Christ the top priority in your life, and let the transformation, both personal and familial, begin!

Family + Time Spent Together = Familial Strength

The second encouragement I would have you consider is your need to spend generous amounts of time with the family God has given you. Few things will strengthen your clan more than time spent together. God designed the family to *live* together.

All too often families find themselves alienated from one another. Mom and dad are busy with their commitments, and the children have their list of "have to" activities. Family members isolate themselves from one another through their busy schedules, and in the end they drift apart. Practically speaking, they cease to be a family unit and resemble strangers living in a boardinghouse. They eat and sleep in the same locality, but they live their lives in other places, with other people.

A typical day for some households in suburbia has all the family warmth and intimacy of an anthill. After a fast paced morning and afternoon spent apart - at work and school – many families scramble through the cupboards and refrigerator for (I guess you would call it) dinner.

With barely enough time to chew, let alone breath – much less talk – in between mouthfuls, these people who share a common last name then crowd into the car and rush off to the practice fields, or other scheduled events, and split apart at the speed of multiple sports and activities.

Dad "stays" with one of the kids at soccer practice and stares at the tiny form of his son from a distant sideline. Ah, nothing like a little father and son bonding time! Meanwhile mom races about town like a monorail. She drops off those strangely familiar children at predetermined unloading points (She has seen them before, she knows she has!) with mind numbing predictability.

No sooner has she dropped off the last of them, she reverses her cycle and inexplicably - like a goose instinctively flies south for the winter – returns to rendezvous with the same small people. Suddenly, recalling the pain of childbirth, she remembers who they are and with a narrow squint returns to pick up the person responsible for the uncomfortable memory – Dad! The vacuum of the short ride home "together" is filled with ear buds, lost in handheld video games, or covered over with the least objectionable form of grown-up music possible – i.e., something everybody can tolerate, just as long as it masks the awkward stillness of laconic conversations.

Once at the house, the weary "family" crawls out of their SUV into their lodging and proceed their separate ways for an hour or two of isolated techno-distractions (iPod, computer, television, video games, etc.). This personal "decompression" time continues until, blacking out, the boarders lose complete consciousness of each other – it's called sleep.

The next day the cycle begins again. Days turn into weeks, weeks into months, and months into precious few years spent increasingly isolated from one another. Sadly, when families drift apart, God's pattern for the family is impossible to implement.

Obviously, that is an embellishment of what busy families know, yet there may be a ring of familiarity in that description. You may say, "We're busy, but not loopy-busy!" You may be newly married, or brand new parents, so you have yet to run into the disintegrating buzz saw of such craziness. You may have activities under control. Perhaps you are determined this will not happen to your family. Good! Others of you are beginning to sense your schedule getting out of hand and potentially out of control.

Regardless of where you are, don't think that your family is *beyond becoming a boardinghouse*. It is always a good idea to evaluate your activities as a family in order to maximize your time together. Parents, it is time spent together that will allow you to develop intimacy with your family and to shepherd them in a manner that pleases the Lord and results in maximum blessing.

It is no coincidence that the greatest parental passage in the Bible, Deuteronomy 6:1-9, commands us to train our children in the ebb and flow of daily life. "These words, which I am commanding you today, shall be on your heart. You shall *teach* them diligently to your sons and shall *talk* of them when you *sit in your house* and when you *walk by the way* and when you *lie down* and when you *rise up*" (Deuteronomy 6:6, 7; emphasis added).

One of the evident realities underlying this passage is the assumption of time spent with our children! The word of God that invades our heart expresses itself in what we teach our children, what we talk about with them, and this constant communication ought to occupy our daily routine, i.e., the waking hours of our day.

Teaching our kids God's wisdom for living, talking to our children about the things of God, should absorb the lion's share of our free time. The biblical imperative to shape our sons and daughters in

God's truth should be the magnetic force that pulls us together as a family for the greatest measure of our day. That same need should help us repel the intrusions that minimize our time together, and therefore weaken the relational bonds of a family, and the spiritual impact parents can have on their children.

This is a priority we need to fight for continually in today's busy world. Parents and children are constantly bombarded by choices that pull them in multiple directions, complicate life, and rob them of the essential time families need to build relationships and grow in God.

The point I'm trying to make is this: spend more time together! Make decisions and choices for your home that will simplify your schedule and result in sharing life. To that end, here are a few suggestions to help you on your way.

Resolve to have dinner as a family several times per week. I've known families for whom dinner together comes around about as often as Christmas. This simply ought not to be!

When we enjoy the company of friends, or seek to know someone more closely, we often share a meal with them. When we celebrate great events in our lives (birthdays, weddings, etc.) we normally do so with food. Why? Because generally we share the table with people we care about, and the experience of eating together takes time and allows us to nurture the relationships we value.

This is why the Bible often portrays people in relationship eating together (Genesis 14:8; 18:1-8; Exodus 10:9; 23:14, 17; Ruth 2:14; Ezra 6:22; Job 1:4; 42:11; Matthew 26:20, 26-29; Mark 14:25; Acts 2:46; Revelation 19:9). Sharing meals helps bring families together and creates a point of contact to talk about life and God.

Make it a habit to worship and serve together. There is a disturbing trend among evangelical families to approach "church and worship" in a piecemeal fashion. Many are choosing "programs" in multiple churches, rather then committing themselves to one local body of believers. Driven by a consumer mindset, parents parcel out their members to fulfill the perceived needs of each. This approach is obviously fraught with many problems (which we cannot discuss at the present time), but at the very least it brings yet another flurry of activity that disengages the individuals of a family from one another.

Our worship of God and our service to the body of Christ is intended to pull us together in unity, and not isolate us from each other. There is much value in the truth that says, "The family that worships and serves together, stays together!"

Play more together instead of apart. That simple statement grates against the common wisdom of the day. We have largely bought into the notion children need to be involved in several sports in order to become well-adjusted adults. Consequently, there is an unrelenting push to get kids incorporated into organized sports so that they can learn the value of teamwork, and experience the thrill of competition, etc. Learning to work with others for a common goal is a valuable skill, and personally I love to compete - I love to win (maybe too much!).

But I truly believe we underestimate the potential to experience such things within the family. It is no secret that a commitment to sports will shorten the time we can spend interacting with each other. I'm not suggesting that organized sports have no place in our familial existence, but we do need to understand that it must be a measured place. Sports – like any other obsession – can greedily swallow up valuable time our families so desperately need.

Regarding organized sports, the high desire some parents have to see their kids compete is a variable that is rarely, fairly evaluated in "The Value of Sports" equation. This factor frequently clouds and degrades many decisions parents make for their children. It must be evaluated honestly by each of us in light of the call and responsibility God places on parents.

One shortsighted judgment I have often observed parents make is what I call the "Yeah, but my kid is special!" assessment. Flushed with an intoxicating awareness of their four-year-olds alacrity on the tyke's soccer field, they commit their little one and family to a lifestyle of childhood sports activities. The cost in time (not to mention money) is high, but they "just sense" their kid will one day garner a scholarship to a division one school, and after all, isn't their education and their future happiness worth the sacrifices they will have to make?

Parents need to guard against this notion, and evaluate the long-term commitments they make for their children. Realistically, only a fraction of participants in the various sports compete at the collegiate level, let alone get a scholarship, let alone get to play, let alone make it to the pros. Unfortunately, these unspoken expectations can lead both parent and child through a long series of disappointments, and potentially to a rocky relationship.

Furthermore, even if a child is gifted in a particular sport, questions that are rarely considered in the decision making process are the obvious ones, "How much will the pursuit of excellence in this sport take my child away from his/her family? How will this impact our priority to worship on Sundays or involve ourselves in ministry? Is my son or daughter rooted well enough in Christ to handle the inordinate praise our culture heaps on the sports icon, or does this "success" pose significant temptations for him/her?"

"Will such a commitment to excel deny him/her too many of the simple joys of childhood (uninterrupted hours of imaginative play with siblings and buddies, knowing the uncomplicated fun of a neighborhood pick up game, playing catch with his/her dad, sleeping in on an occasional Saturday, having the freedom on a whim to go somewhere special with a friend, or his/her family, etc., etc., etc.)?"

Organized sports can have a place in your family's lifestyle, but before you pledge your child, your family to sporting activities, I encourage you to prayerfully evaluate your commitments. I would urge you to count the cost.

One delightful way to spend more time together is to simply play together. Over the course of the last twenty years our family has spent countless hours laughing, talking, bantering (exchanging sanctified "jaw"), and enjoying one another's fellowship over a household game, playing in the pool, or mixing it up at the ping pong table. The casual interplay of leisure has provided the platform for many a thoughtful discussion. Yes, playing together will demanded a sizable chunk of your free time, but this investment in one another will help make your home a place where your kids love to be.

Read as a clan – One of the most valuable ways to come together as a family is around a great book. Don't underestimate the power of reading a compelling book aloud. There are some who would object and declare this an outmoded form from a by-gone era. 'It belongs with the radio and the Model-T. Today's children are much too sophisticated to be engaged by reading aloud.'

I respectfully disagree. Nothing can capture the imagination like a good book, and to be able to take a journey in your mind accompanied by the ones you love is an extraordinary experience that leaves participants wanting more. It engages everyone's mind and heart and stimulates conversation and inquiry.

In my travels across this country to speak, I have taken my family with me as much as finances allow. We live in Southern California so whenever I am asked to speak to a group west of the Rockies, I try to drive to get some extended time with my wife and children. We have chalked up some prodigious miles over the last fifteen years and almost as many memories. Usually our traveling adventures compose the highlight(s) of our year, and without exception our favorite pastime on the road is listening to my wife read a great book.

We have read stacks of Christian books and classic literature during our winding road hours. Some books were better than others, a number were didactic in nature, while many arrested our attention with spellbinding plots, or personal accounts of great adventures. Each book, in one way or another, captivated my entire family and proved to be a joy in its own right. All of them have made us think and led to discussions we would not have had otherwise.

I suppose the greatest benefit of "road-reading" for all of us continues to be the extended fellowship we experience as parents and children. I'm not speaking of time spent in the same cabin compartment isolated from one another, but hours fully engaged with each other as a family. Certainly long drives are a prime opportunity to enjoy a good book in a shared space. Next time you have a good stretch in the car, try reading a book! It sure beats plugging in the opiate of a DVD after every restroom stop. I believe reading creates a hearth-like environment regardless of the immediate context.

Obviously, you don't have to take long trips in a car to enjoy the reading experience. There are several ways you can gather your loved ones around a great book be it a fictional story, a biography (missionary biographies make riveting reading), or an historical event or period (such as the migration of the Puritans to the American continent).[9] Dedicate one hour, one night a week to reading as a family, or read for fifteen to twenty minutes after dinner two to three times per week.

This is what we are doing at this time; we are savoring the autobiography of C. H. Spurgeon, a little bite at a time – kind of like dessert.

This past spring break we packed up the family car and traveled north to see the majestic California Redwoods. It was the only opportunity we would have to enjoy Joshua (our eldest) for an extended trip all year. He was wrapping up a brutal quarter at the University of California, Irvine (21 units of chemistry, physics, mathematics, and research!), and we were looking forward to many hours of unbroken fellowship with our entire family. Traveling up the length of the stunning California coastal valleys and rugged shoreline, my wife Valorie began to read to her captive audience. She started in on Gene Stratton-Porter's excellent book, "The Keeper of The Bees."

As usual, my children continued coaxing their mother to read on, especially Joshua. It's a 536 page book and so Valorie read, and read, and read until her voice and the California Coastline said "enough!" After a moderate first day's drive (nine hours, moderate for us) we arrived just south of the San Francisco Bay and put up for the night. Once we were settled in our room I turned to the kids and asked, "Guys, it's still early. What do you want to do?"

I suggested we cool off at the pool, go for a walk and take some pictures, or perhaps just chill for a while in our comfortable air-conditioned room with a favorite DVD. In answer to my inquiry my 22-year-old college student spoke first and said, "You know dad, if it's all the same to everyone, I would just assume have mom read more." The vote was unanimous, and my hoarse wife could not deny the enthusiastic request.

Both Valorie and I were struck by that moment. You would think that a college student about to launch into a chemistry Ph.D. would have little interest in joining his parents and younger siblings in a family reading time. Yet he was the one who suggested it and swayed the vote. The enjoyment and interaction this activity can produce over the years is immeasurable. Don't cave in to the media fed perception that reading cannot interest children and teenagers. It is a powerful tool to bring your family together.

One Final Thought About Our Simple Equation: Time + Family = Strength

Here's the operative word for the above suggestions, "*evaluate*" your lifestyle in view of your need to *live* together. It is amazing how quickly our lives can become cluttered with worldly influences and a preponderance of frenetic and distracting activities. It is wise to evaluate where you and your family invest the precious time God allots to you. In light of that, please consider the following questions and statements.

Determine what worldly attitudes/values, if any, need to change in your family (e.g., is there an inordinate longing for the "stuff" of this world, a desire to win at all cost, lack of appreciation for God's greatest gifts – salvation, family, church, etc.)?

What values, activities, nonessential commitments pull your family in different directions and cause you to drift apart?

Pinpoint these things with your spouse and children. Make a list, lay it out on the kitchen table and discuss it with your entire family.

Identify the activities and commitments that can be reduced, or eliminated. I have yet to meet one family that regrets having spent more time together, but I have met many who mourn the lost opportunities and unhealthy relationships created by the passing distractions of this world. Evaluate your time commitments outside of the home, and do what you must do to spend more time together as a household.

A FEW WORDS OF APPLICATION FOR THE CHRISTIAN HOME

PART TWO

Considerations and Questions for Parents

If possible answer these questions and discuss your answers with your spouse or a trusted Christian friend.

Identify an area or two where you have succeeded in leading your children spiritually (e.g., teaching them to pray; biblically counseling them through a life crisis - death, illness – or shepherding them through the gospel to salvation; teaching them to treasure God's promises).

Q. What did you say/do to help them?

Q. What do you think made your shepherding particularly effective for your child/children?

Q. What biblical promises and/or instruction did you find particularly helpful in guiding your children through their experience?

Q. Presently, what is the biggest challenge – or challenges - you face in guiding your children through life (e.g., leading them to salvation; teaching them consistent obedience; helping them work through a particular weakness such as anger, ingratitude, anxiety; walking them through their relationships with the opposite sex; encouraging them in their own relationship with their spouse and/or parenting, etc.).

Q. *Where* and *how* does the Bible address the challenges you face?

Here's a simple exercise that will help lead you to some biblical answers for the parenting questions you encounter.

1) First, define your challenges down to a few key terms, or a single word. For instance, using the examples above: *Leading someone to salvation*, key terms would include - gospel, sin, sinners, believe, faith, salvation, eternal life; *Teaching your young ones consistent obedience* - obedience, obey; *Helping them work through a particular weakness such as anger* – anger, angry, wrath; *ingratitude – ungrateful*, grumble, grateful, thankful, thankfulness; *anxiety* - anxious, worry; *Walking your teens through their relationships with the opposite sex* - purity, purify (to avoid getting bogged down in Old Testament ceremonial laws, with certain terms such as "purify," pay particular attention to New Testament references), purifies, lust, unmarried, sisters, married, marriage; etc. Perhaps you are dealing with an entirely different question, or set of circumstances. The key thing is to identify it (them) in order to search the scripture for God's counsel regarding your needs.

2) Using your *concordance*, search for your key terms, look up these passages and read them in context. I suggest you employ the *cross-reference* tool in the margins (or middle) of your Bible to find additional scriptures dealing with your subject of interest. If you don't have a Bible with a reference tool, I would strongly encourage you to purchase one. It will provide you with a valuable asset in searching the scripture.

3) List the key shepherding challenges you face one by one. Next to each one of these write down the particular scriptures that address your concern - either directly (*Obedience*, Ephesians 6:1, "Children, obey your parents in the Lord, for this is right."), or in principle (*Anger*, Numbers 20:1-13, the account when Moses became angry with the people, and struck the rock in disobedience).

4) Next, carefully consider these scriptures in context to determine what they teach. What is the principle, or what are the principles these scriptures teach regarding the issues or questions you face as a parent? Write out a summary of your answers.

Don't hesitate to ask a faithful pastor, a reputable church leader, or Christian friend who is skilful in handling the word of God for help and wisdom in your quest to understand God's word.

5) Finally, as you come to understand the texts that speak to your issues, ask yourself, "In light of what God has said, what must I do practically to improve the spiritual oversight of my children? How do these principles apply to my particular situation? What must I do to implement this biblical truth into my life and/or the life of my children?" Keep a journal of your questions, answers, and resolves. Make your action steps a focus of your petitions before the Lord and share them with your spouse.

CHAPTER SIX

Innocence Assailed

The marriage union and the parent/child relationship are two high profile targets in the enemy's war against the family, but there is a third less evident target often left unprotected by unsuspecting parents. I am speaking of the battle for the innocence, the sexual purity of young people. Perhaps we assume that our children are less likely than others to succumb to sexual temptation. If that is your assumption, it is an extremely dangerous one.

Not only are our children fallen sons and daughters of Adam, they are the targets of an intensified barrage of sexual bombardment such as the world has never seen. I beg you to take the following, brief but sober warning to heart because it poses a very real threat to your children and your family. My heart's desire is for all of us to be aware of the imminent danger surrounding our families, so that we may be delivered from one of the greatest evils of our lifetime.

"However, if you have warned the righteous man that the righteous should not sin and he does not sin, he shall surely live because he took warning; and you have delivered yourself" (Ezekiel 3:21).

The Moral Degradation of Young People

The enemy takes his fight to the family on a third and crucial front; it is the battleground for the purity of our children. Most of us have encountered people whose sexual appetites have careened out of control. Many of us could tell the tragic stories of men and women who shipwrecked their lives and families on the shoals of uncontrolled passions.

Without exception, every person I have met in such dire conditions can trace their disastrous behavior to patterns developed in the early years of life. Proceeding in their thoughts and habits without parental accountability – and therefore without much protection – they continued down a calamitous path of assured destruction.

I realize that not every person who destroys his, or her life through sexual sin does so because of a parent's neglect. Each man and woman is accountable to God for their own behavior regardless of personal history, but obviously the failure of parents to protect their children from sexual seduction predisposes them to a ruinous end.

The earlier the enemy ensnares a young person through sexual sin, the more likely he will be able to corrupt them for life and potentially harden them to the gospel. Realize this, the plan of the enemy is to ensnare and enslave people, and the earlier he can achieve this aim, the more damage he will inflict on a soul. Certainly, sexual temptation has been a danger for humanity since the fall, but the audacious nature of the enemy's warring on this battleground - over the last several decades - poses a peril for our young people like never before.

Perhaps more today than at any other time in our modern history (the last 60 years), the enemy has focused his twisted schemes on the tender years of youth; His goal, to corrupt the innocence of our young. His strategy is to pollute our young men and women sexually. What is particularly alarming is he has progressively targeted younger and younger children with devastating success.

Be it through the media, the indoctrination of secular education, misguided legislation, pop-culture - and usually under the banner of "Freedom!" - children have been marked out for moral corruption at an ever younger age. This is what I have termed "the sexualization of children" and it is a fight for the souls of the young. It is nothing less than a cunning, demonic scheme to enslave and harden humanity in the blossom of life.

The reality parents must face is that this is a cosmic struggle, a chosen and favorite battleground for the devil to conduct his destructive mischief. As parents, we must protect our children from the evil onslaught they face continually from multiple, deadly, and increasingly effective stratagems.

The Pervasive Presence of Our Struggle

This pervasive attempt to sexualize children was vividly driven home to us recently through the seemingly innocuous chore of shopping. Visiting a nationally recognized family department store, my wife decided to check out children's clothes for the upcoming fall. Rummaging through the girls clothing section she discovered a line of T-shirts targeting girls in middle school to high school. What she saw printed on these T's shocked her.

The line of garments featured pithy, little phrases designed to draw attention to the wearer. Normally you would expect to find monikers suitable for twelve and thirteen year old girls, or familiar icons like Mini Mouse impressed on such gear. Instead the statements emblazoned on these pieces read like the fulfillment of Romans 1:28-32. Examine Paul's words and then compare them to the deplorable declarations printed on these clothing items.

"And just as they did not see fit to acknowledge God any longer, God gave them over to a depraved mind, to do those things which are not proper, being filled with all unrighteousness, wickedness, greed, evil; full of envy, murder, strife, deceit, malice; they are gossips, slanderers, haters of God, insolent, arrogant, boastful, inventors of evil, disobedient to parents, without understanding, untrustworthy, unloving, unmerciful; and although they know the ordinance of God, that those who practice such things are worthy of death, they not only do the same, but also give hearty approval to those who practice them."

Most of the statements brandished on the tops were sexual in nature, so be forewarned, and keep in mind this apparel targeted girls as young as 11 and 12. The line of back-to-school clothes heralded the following audacities and attitudes: "Spicy Number," "Totally Twisted," "My parents think I'm studying," "Dump Him – Mission Accomplished," "More me … less you," "Get out of my space," "Loserville," "This is what love looks like," "I'm the naughty sister," "I can barely stand you," "U Bug Me," "Don't ever try 'cause you'll never get it," "You have 00 chance with me," "I just realized I don't care," "It's all about me," "I'm very good at being bad," "Let's download something naughty."

That's a far cry from Mini Mouse and a lot like the description Paul gives us of hardened sinners. Again, these items are marketed to preteens and teens. This line of garments is an expression of the sexually loaded poison aimed at our young people. Frankly, I am amazed that this type of garbage actually sells. Even more bewildering still is the thought that parents actually purchase this morally twisted poison for their daughters!

Granted, not many people reading this book would ever even consider buying such filth for their girls. However, we need to recognize that this is the kind of message our young people constantly encounter when they step out into the public arena. Just visit your neighborhood mall, listen to pop music, or thumb through a fashion magazine and the message to young people becomes evidently clear, "You are your own authority. You're master over your own body. Explore your sexuality. Live as you want! ... And oh yes, don't forget, 'be careful' (the politically correct, feel-good caveat, of the libertine progressives)!" The fallen culture in which we live relentlessly foists this injurious lie on children with ruinous results.

The call to unrestrained sexual expression is one of the incessant drumbeats of our modern world to the emerging generation, and while it promises freedom and pleasure, it guarantees nothing less than the assured corruption and destruction of young lives. We must be ready to identify and confront this falsehood in whatever form we see it, and to arm our children with God's mind so they may resist and flee from the lure of the devil.

God's desire for believing young people is clear and stands in contradiction to the seduction of this present age. "For this is the will of God, your sanctification; that is, that you abstain from sexual immorality" (1 Thessalonians 4:3); "Submit therefore to God. Resist the devil and he will flee from you" (James 4:7).

Much of the war on the family rages in these critical areas, the attack against the sacred union between husband and wife, the assault to undermine the parent/child relationship, and the assailing of children's innocence. Mark these essential arenas for protection because you can be certain that the enemy has marked them out for destruction.

CHAPTER SEVEN

Incoming Missiles!

We have considered three essential battlefronts on which the war on the family rages. The world aims to destroy the marriage union, it seeks to undermine the relationship between parents and their offspring, and endeavors to corrupt the innocence of children. Without doubt, it is important to comprehend where to fight the fight, but it is equally critical to be aware of the weapons employed against us so we may counter with a biblical response. This leads us to ask the obvious question, "What are some of the predominant means by which the enemy attacks the family today?"

One thing we can say with certainty is the enemy's attack on the home is manifold, but the schemes fall into general categories such as the two we will discuss in the following pages. They represent two broad range of missiles aimed at our homes for the purpose of their destruction. There are other types of weaponry employed but here are two dominant categories through which secular culture besieges the family. They are, the ubiquitous entertainment industry and an irreligious, humanistic educational system.

The Entertainment Media

One of the most seditious assaults on our families comes from the entertainment media, i.e., popular literature, television/film industries, and the contemporary music business.

To catalog the anti-family message produced by the entertainment industry would take several volumes. It would most assuredly engulf this entire book, and take a research staff the size of the Human Genome Project to pull off. So without being too copious allow me to illustrate the relentless attack by these entities on our homes with a simple exercise, and a few straightforward questions.

Rather than make an extended grocery list of anti-family entertainment, make a mental count of media examples in your recent experience that have affirmed an accurate, biblical view of the family. I would suggest you do this with your spouse, perhaps even your children.

Ask yourself, "How many TV shows, movies, songs, secular books, etc. have I seen/heard/read in the last two years that extol biblical values in the home?" Biblical virtues such as:

- Sexual purity

- A joyous monogamous marriage

- A family where the dad – far from being a clueless 'wuss' – humbly and courageously leads his family

- A home that portrays a happy, submissive wife

- A mother who is singularly devoted to her family rather than a career outside the home

- A home that positively portrays submission-obedience-humility-modesty in children

- Siblings that genuinely love one another

- Family members that forgive each other even at great cost

- Families that enjoy being with one another

- Families that exhibit kindness, forbearance, selflessness toward one another

- A show/movie suggesting a family goes to church together - without making them out to be the Taliban.

I challenge you to make a list of secular entertainment experiences where virtuous families—families modeling the virtues in the above paragraph—have been the focal point. Here's a challenging twist, try to focus on the contemporary entertainment media. This exercise will be hard to do without going back to "The Andy Griffith Show," "Father Knows Best" (talk about a politically incorrect title for today's Hollywood?!), or "The Waltons."

Needless to say, your list of examples is going to be pretty short. In fact, if you were to turn the previous list of family virtues into a suggestion list for the creative gurus of the entertainment media, and take it to them as a jumping point for next year's pop songs, TV schedule, movie offerings, and best sellers, they would think you were mad! What a terrifically boring and out of touch set of ideas to portray!!!

Show up to the Burbank studios with such a list and the response would likely be, "Where's the intrigue without betrayal and a racy illicit relationship? Dad as the "strong leader," and mom as just a... a mother? In a submissive supporting role no less? What, are you some kind of misogynist? Modesty? How do you spell that? What is that? How can we expect people to watch if we don't show them something, unless we titillate their imaginations with forbidden fruit?"

In today's secular entertainment media, biblical virtue and a principled home does not sell, and so families are bombarded with the antithesis of what the Bible extols. Unfortunately, this is what we often bring into our homes. I'm not trying to be the "Purity Police," nor would

I have you become legalistic and paranoid about the contemporary entertainment industry.

That said, we do need to protect our families from the hostilities of this world. We must exercise wise discernment about what we allow into our homes, and it is important that we debrief with our children when we encounter messages that contradict God's principles for our lives.

We must continually protect, correct, and instruct our household in God's truth. God's word is a shield to us that will safeguard our homes from the destructive toxins of this world. If we don't use the sentinel of God's word to protect the family, the corrosive elements of this world's way of thinking will eat away at our family's integrity until it is morally compromised.

That is the enemy's "end game" for your home: compromise and ultimate destruction. We would do well to remember, however, that a family's ruin does not generally happen as a result of one catastrophic event, rather its destruction is the culmination of a long string of moral, biblical compromises that end in ruin.

The corrupt thinking of this world weakens a family much like a corrosive works on a bridge. Generally environmental agents, like the salt sea air, do their work a little at a time, imperceptibly at first but progressively nonetheless until a system or a structure is compromised and then collapses.

One of the thrills we experienced in our family travels last year was crossing the famed Golden Gate Bridge on a beautiful, sunny San Francisco afternoon. The sun doesn't always smile on the orange colossus, so we were ecstatic to see the Golden Gate Bridge in all her vibrant glory. I was awed by the grandeur and beauty of the nostalgic structure, and as we crossed its massive expanse I gave a fleeting thought to the integrity of the bridge. My thought was "fleeting" because I knew that a team of engineers and specialists continually fuss over this favorite California icon. They are literally all over that bridge like ugly on ape, like paint on a … well, like paint on a bridge. They have to be!

The stunning, azure San Francisco Bay is ruggedly beautiful, but it is an unfriendly environment for a heavy metal bridge. The cold, damp fog and ever-present high salt content in the air would destroy the bridge over time if it were not for the vigilant caretakers that brood over the structure like a mother bear watches over her cubs. Since its creation, the bridge has been painted completely only three times - primarily to thwart the effects of advancing corrosion and to comply with environmental concerns - but it is in a perpetual state of repair due to the invasive nature of the damp salt air.

In 2008, the team of Golden Gate caretakers began the gargantuan process of completely restoring the main cables. This is on top of the ongoing painting and sundry maintenance projects on the 70 year old pride of San Francisco. There is a constant buzz of maintenance to keep the bridge not only beautiful, but more importantly, strong and safe.[1]

What do you think would happen if the city of San Francisco left the Golden Gate Bridge to the devouring elements of the bay? How long do you think the bridge would survive? Perhaps a long time, it is after all a well-built structure designed to last. Even so, abandoned to the unrelenting corrosives of the sea, the bridge would slowly - imperceptibly at first yet inevitably - rust away. Then one day, compromised at critical stress points, the grand old structure would simply collapse under the strain of its own prodigious weight.

Parents are the watchmen, caretakers of their families, their children, the souls entrusted to their care. The lies and sin of this world are bitter corrosives to our souls and the wellbeing of our families. Like diligent watchmen we must be careful to constantly protect our homes from the damaging elements so glibly offered to us by the contemporary entertainment media. If we're not dutiful in this responsibility, then we are potentially setting up our marriages, children, families for moral collapse. It may not happen overnight, but continual, unguarded exposure to the lies and filth of this age will have devastating consequences for our families.

Perhaps a good rubric to follow regarding our standards for entertainment would be the words of David in Psalm 101:2, 3. "I will give heed to the blameless way . . . I will walk within my house in the integrity of my heart. I will set no worthless thing before my eyes; I hate the work of those who fall away; it shall not fasten its grip on me."

While we may be able to protect our families from some of the harmful effects of the media industry, we cannot avoid the ever-present evil in the world. Getting rid of your TV, etc. is simply not going to deliver you from the pervasive malignancy that saturates a reprobate culture. We will encounter evil everywhere we turn, and that evil will militate against the spiritual health of our homes.

This means we must be ever watchful over our homes, sober and alert (1 Peter 5:8) having our senses trained by the word of God and obedience, to discern the corrupting influences of the enemy and the evil that is in this world.

"For everyone who partakes only of milk is not accustomed to the word of righteousness, for he is an infant. But solid food is for the mature, who because of practice have their senses trained to discern good and evil" (Hebrews 5:13, 14).

Secular Education

A caveat is immediately in order before we proceed on this point. Let me say straight out that I recognize there are many excellent educators in the public schools who excel in their craft and who do not share the political/philosophical views of many of their policymakers. Most of us can testify to a handful of teachers whose knowledge of a subject, genuine enthusiasm for teaching and personal care for their students impacted us.

There are also Christian teachers and administrators in public education who endeavor faithfully to be salt and light to their fellow educators and pupils. I have known several excellent Christian educators through the years. The issue I desire to address in this section has very little to do with conscientious professionals, teaching styles, etc. The concern we will discuss is the anti-family ideology directing the overall course of present day public education.

One of the means utilized by the enemy to undermine the institution of the family is the contemporary, secular educational system. Once again, I don't mean to imply that all public education aims to torpedo the family, but there has been a growing effort by the pedagogical elite to indoctrinate children with secular values, as well as to educate them in the basic academic disciplines (reading, writing, and arithmetic).

Much of the secular values directed toward children are framed by an aggressive agenda to redefine what is sexually acceptable. As I pointed out previously, this is a battlefield of choice in the devil's ongoing war against the institution of the family.

If the enemy can redefine what is sexually acceptable through the educational system, he can indoctrinate, reprogram, corrupt the lives of a generation, and obliterate God's ordained pattern for the family (one man for one woman, exercising loving authority and direction in the lives of their obedient children) from culture.

Make no mistake about it, there is an active secular agenda shaping modern education. It is embraced at high levels (policymakers) and eventually works its way down to the classroom. Take for example the powerful influence of the National Education Association (NEA). The NEA is the most powerful teachers union in the United States. It is extremely liberal and financially supports advocacy groups such as the Rainbow PUSH Coalition, the Gay and Lesbian Alliance Against Defamation, and Amnesty International among others.[2]

What the support of these left-wing organizations has to do with the academic preparation of children is beyond me. What it does reveal however is the NEA is interested in much more than improving the academic state of children. Its support for left-wing causes discloses its radical ideology, and the liberal political agenda it promotes to undermine the traditional family by proxy (radical advocacy groups, liberal legislators). It seeks radical social change, not just traditional education.

The NEA advances an equally "progressive" ideology in education itself. Endowed with impressive financial wherewithal and the political power surrendered to it by its massive rank and file, the NEA foists its liberal philosophy and influence on the public school system. Reporting for Eagle Forum, Phyllis Schlafly summarizes the unabashed left-wing agenda put forth by the NEA at the 2006 National Convention. She writes,

"Other NEA resolutions promote the gay rights agenda in public school curricula by demanding funds to alleviate "sexual orientation discrimination," to use multicultural education to reduce "homophobia," (i.e., *an attempt to link legitimate ethnic civil rights with gay rights*; emphasis added) and even to put "diversity-based curricula" and "bias-free screening devices in early childhood education." She continues,

"NEA resolutions again endorse the principal goals of the feminist agenda, including abortion, the Equal Rights Amendment, Comparable Worth, nonsexist language, and a federally funded women's commission to pursue feminist goals at taxpayers' expense. The NEA also supports "community-operated, school-based family planning clinics that will provide intensive counseling," which is a thinly veiled welcome to Planned Parenthood to put its clinics in the schools.[3]

Most parents (Christian and traditional Americans) don't feel the aforementioned NEA politics and policies reflect their own values and would strongly object to having their children programmed with such counter-conscience indoctrination. This is exactly why secular education also seeks to diminish, ignore, circumvent, or simply suppress the concerns and authority of parents to implement their avant-garde values agenda.[4]

Some might call the discussion above "Alarmist!" and object, "Educational bureaucrats will banter philosophically with such ideas among themselves, but that kind of stuff doesn't make its way down to the classroom. Educators would never try to impose these ideas over the objection of parents. The article sighted above was a report on the 2006 NEA National Convention. Here we are two plus years later. Where's the evidence of this aggressive, moral reconstruction in the schools?"

Unfortunately, this type of indoctrination is a present day reality in public schools across the nation. In fact, it has become more evident in these last years as policy expresses its way through the system. For example, prior to the 2006 NEA convention, in the spring of 2005, a Massachusetts father raised objections over a book issued in his son's kindergarten class. The book was designed to teach five year olds about homosexuality. This father's conscientious objections eventually got him arrested and placed in jail for the night. Gratefully the charges were later dropped, but the conflict illustrates the high-handed, parent-circumventing agenda employed across much of our country.

On October 20, 2005 the World Net Daily reported on the incident mentioned above, "The dispute began last spring when (David) Parker's then-5-year-old son brought home a book to be shared with his parents titled, "Who's in a Family?" The optional reading material, which came in a "Diversity Book Bag," depicted at least two households led by homosexual partners."

"The illustrated book says, "A family can be made up in many different ways" and includes this text: "Laura and Kyle live with their two moms, Joyce and Emily, and a poodle named Daisy. It takes all four of them to give Daisy her bath." Another illustrated page says: "Robin's family is made up of her dad, Clifford, her dad's partner, Henry, and Robin's cat, Sassy. Clifford and Henry take turns making dinner for their family.""

"Parker complained to school officials, and at a scheduled meeting at Estabrook Elementary School April 27 with the principal and the town's director of education, he was told an agreement could be reached. But after the superintendent intervened via telephone, Parker abruptly was told that unless he left the meeting he would be arrested. Parker insisted that an agreement be reached before he left, and school officials called police, who handcuffed him and brought him to jail, where he spent the night."[5]

In 2007, the State Legislature of Colorado approved a proposal put forth by representative Nancy Todd requiring schools to teach children how to use condoms. In an interview with the Rocky Mountain News, a fellow legislator stated that this proposal would result in a "…comprehensive condom, contraceptive, and copulation course of study for all students."[6]

Just this year in the same week, in the state of Illinois and once again in Massachusetts, two outrageous school sponsored events captured headlines. Both schools sponsored gay awareness events while at the same time circumventing the parents of the children involved. In fact, parents were prohibited from attending. Bob Unruh of the World Net Daily reported,

"Administrators at North Newton High School in Newton, Mass., have held a seminar for students that explained how to know they are homosexual, but banned parents from attending … The event, called "ToBeGlad Day," was the school's 'Transgender Bisexual Gay Awareness Day'," and students were given a pamphlet that explains what it means to be "gay," tells students how they are supposed to know if they are "gay," and responds to the question, "Will I ever have sex? … some of the topics of the seminar, as reported by the student newspaper, included: "It's natural to be gay," "Nature vs. Nurture," and "Fabulous Gay History." … A second brochure included 16 pages of website addresses, telephone numbers and other information through which the students can reach "gay" organizations, law firms, advocacy groups, and support clubs … News of the event comes just a day after WND reported on a case at Deerfield High School in Deerfield, Ill., where school officials ordered their 14-year-old freshmen class into a "gay" indoctrination seminar, after having them sign a confidentiality agreement promising not to tell their parents."[7]

In my own state of California governor Arnold Schwarzenegger signed bill SB777 into law on October 12, 2007. To be sure this is one of the most troublesome pieces of legislation I have ever witnessed. This bill in effect disallows the use of such terms as "mom and dad," "father and mother," "husband and wife" in the public schools without mentioning alternative possibilities for marriage and parenting. Traditional titles such as "mom and dad" are now deemed discriminatory to kids and teachers who are homosexual, bisexual, transgender, etc.

SB777 also prescribes that schools accommodate kids who are gender sensitive. What does that mean? The bill mandates that schools allow boys to use the girls' bathrooms/locker rooms (and vice versa) if their gender identity compels them to. Additionally, this legislative gem decrees that homecoming queens and kings can now be either male or female, setting up the potential irony - and awkward moment - of having a male homecoming queen paired with a female homecoming king. Ludicrous? Yes, but any traditional view of male female roles without making allowances for alternative lifestyles would be considered "discriminatory" by the state of California.

The harsh reality of this is legislation is inescapable. Again, Bob Unruh describes this very thing in an article written shortly after Governor Schwarzenegger signed the bill into law, "...SB777...bans anything in public schools that could be interpreted as negative toward homosexuality, bisexuality and other alternative lifestyle choices."

Quoting Randy Thomasson (president of Campaign for Children and Families, who fought the bill vigorously) the article continues, "SB777 prohibits any "instruction" or school-sponsored "activity" that "promotes a discriminatory bias" against "gender" – the bill's definition includes cross-dressing and sex changes – as well as "sexual orientation." Because no textbook or instruction in California public schools currently disparages transsexuality, bisexuality, or homosexuality, the practical effect of SB777 will be to require positive portrayals of these sexual lifestyles at every government-operated school," … Offenders will face the wrath of the state Department of Education, up to and including lawsuits."

The motivation behind this legislation is ostensibly to counteract discrimination, but since there are no identical protections in the law for students holding to a traditional view of the family, this law effectively discriminates against students and teachers who believe in God's pattern for the home. The WND article continues,

"CCF noted that now on a banned list will be any text, reference or teaching aid that portrays marriage as only between a man and woman, materials that say people are born male or female (and not in between), sources that fail to include a variety of transsexual, bisexual and homosexual historical figures, and sex education materials that fail to offer the option of sex changes."

The actual teeth of SB777 resides in the sister bill the governor signed on the same day, AB394. This bill according to CCF, as quoted by WND "creates the circumstances where a parent who says marriage is only for a man and a woman in the presence of a lesbian teacher could be convicted of "harassment," and a student who believes people are born either male or female could be reported as a "harasser" by a male teacher who wears women's clothes … "

If you believe these are laws that will affect only parents and children living in California you are wrong. Not only do these laws set a precedent for other states, it will embolden the NEA nationally as well as liberal elements in other legislatures to follow suit. Furthermore, there is a financial facet in the fallout of this bill. Unruh points out, "Analysts have warned that schools across the nation will be impacted by the decision, since textbook publishers must cater to their largest purchaser, which often is California, and they will be unlikely to go to the expense of having a separate edition for other states."[8]

These accounts represent a smattering of examples that expose the secular indoctrination children are put through in the arena of public education. This is a reality school children face in manifold ways. And of course I have not touched on the constant rain of relativism with which they are bombarded in the classroom, nor the ubiquitous presence of evolutionary theory and philosophy, nor the pressure they face from peers who buy into the world's value system. This is the real world situation many children come up against day in and day out.

Get Involved!

If your children are in a traditional school setting (public or private) I exhort you to conscientiously, tenaciously, biblically fight for their hearts and minds. Make doubly sure they are strengthened with the "the pure milk of the word, so that by it... (they) may grow in respect to salvation" (1 Peter 2:2). Make it your ambition to know what they are taught in their classrooms.

I encourage you to attend PTA meetings, talk to their teachers, ask questions, look through their textbooks, and dialogue with your children about what they are exposed to on a weekly, if not daily basis. Communicate constantly with your children so that you may be able to discern and biblically combat any message that contradicts scripture and a Christian worldview. If your children participate in a traditional school, it is your duty to continually dialogue and debrief with them about their education. It is your responsibility – as it is of all parents before the Lord – to keep a vigilant pulse on their moral and spiritual wellbeing.

Some might tell you this kind of parental behavior is nosy and intrusive because, after all, the shaping of young minds belongs to professional educators. Nothing could be further from the truth. Children are a stewardship from God to parents, and as such, parents are responsible before the Lord for their spiritual and intellectual development (Ephesians 6:4). It is your obligation to involve yourself in your child's training regardless of the educational system you choose, public school, private school, or homeschool.

Perhaps you are thinking that exercising such vigilance over a child's education is simply too much work. If this is what you believe, it is the equivalent of saying that what your children learn, and subsequently believe is not all that important. The logical consequences of this way of thinking are disastrous. We must employ careful supervision over what others teach our children, and biblically affirm or correct the instruction they receive. If we fail to do that, then we fail to shepherd our children and we are gambling with the eternal treasure God has entrusted to us.

CHAPTER EIGHT

Is Withdrawing from the World the Answer?

The world we live in can be a vexing and oppressive place for those who love God and treasure the institution of the family He has established. The desire to protect our homes from the corruption that is in this world is natural and commendable for Christian parents. It is evidence of the Holy Spirit working through the leadership of dad and mom to safeguard the home.

There are way too many Christian parents who have acclimated to the moral turpitude of our day, and therefore are lulled into moral torpidity by it. The flame of desire to protect the Christian family needs to be fanned, not doused.

We must arm ourselves to that end with God's truth, reinforce our convictions with obedience, hedge our families about with prayer, and surround ourselves with the encouragement and accountability of fellow Christians. Protecting our families from evil is a virtue; however, and we must understand this, isolation is not. Isolating our homes from the world is not a solution for believers, and it is not a firewall against sin.

Boycotting modern civilization and moving to Siberia will not protect your family from the corruption of our present age. Neither can we barricade ourselves in cloistered communes and shut ourselves off from the world in order to preserve our homes from an increasingly secular culture. Unfortunately, some feel isolationism is the answer to the corruption we face in society, yet this is never a viable remedy to ward off evil influence. Living righteously in the midst of an evil day is.

Paul reminded the waffling Corinthians that God desired their practical sanctification from the world in which they lived. God wills that we should live holy lives. He wrote, "Therefore, COME OUT FROM THEIR MIDST AND BE SEPARATE," says the Lord. "AND DO NOT TOUCH WHAT IS UNCLEAN; And I will welcome you" (2 Corinthians 6:17).

In a similar manner the apostle Peter encouraged the dispersed church with these words, "But you are A CHOSEN RACE, A royal PRIESTHOOD, A HOLY NATION, A PEOPLE FOR *God's* OWN POSSESSION." God's saints[1] are a holy people who must set themselves apart from the evil of the day, but – and this is just as important - not from the people who need deliverance from it. That's why Peter ends the verse above with a purpose clause and declares, "*so that* you may proclaim the excellencies of Him who has called you out of darkness into His marvelous light" (1 Peter 2:9, emphasis added).

We have been saved from sin, and set apart to live righteously so that we may call people out of the very evil in which we were once enslaved. For the sake of God's redemptive cause, we cannot isolate our families from unbelieving people. Neither can we confuse withdrawal with obedience to God.

We have been called out of this sinful world to be sure, but we have not yet been collected from it (John 17:15). This will come via death or translation to heaven in accordance with the Lord's good timing, but until that day dawns we must put our lives, our families on display as a testimony of God's grace to a lost humanity.

Sequestering ourselves from the world in which we live is wrong for two reasons, the most important being that by so doing we play right into the enemy's hand. The net effect of removing ourselves from culture is our families cease to be stages where the gospel is dramatically played out for men, women, and children to see.

In effect, instead of becoming salt and light to a decaying and lost world, we remove the salt from that which decays, and we hide the light from the encroaching shadows, leaving the world to perish in darkness (Matthew 5:13-16). We need to protect our children to be sure, but we need to display God's grace to the world through our families.

If the devil can silence Christian families through sin and moral failure or by fear and withdrawal, the net effect is sadly similar: perishing people are deprived of the gospel. Without someone sharing the gospel how will they be saved? Paul posed a similar question to believers in Rome.

In Romans 10:13-15, 17 we read, "for "WHOEVER WILL CALL ON THE NAME OF THE LORD WILL BE SAVED." What a thrilling and gracious promise this is! However, such truth begs a logical series of questions. Paul continues, "How then will they call on Him in whom they have not believed? How will they believe in Him whom they have not heard? And how will they hear without a preacher? How will they preach unless they are sent?" The obvious answer is we must go and proclaim the gospel so that people may believe and be saved. "Just as it is written, "HOW BEAUTIFUL ARE THE FEET OF THOSE WHO BRING GOOD NEWS OF GOOD THINGS!" … So faith comes from hearing, and hearing by the word of Christ."

Remember, the family has a central place in God's redemptive program. God uses the family as an effective delivery system for the gospel. We honor God's truth and the gospel with godly families (Titus 2:3-5). People are drawn to the reality of the saving message by the righteous integrity of our homes and lives, and this opens a door for us to share God's message of life in Jesus Christ.

The Lord Jesus saved us, and when He did He did not immediately usher us into His presence in heaven. Why? Because He has a passion to save the lost of this world, and He accomplishes that grand and gracious task, not through angels, nor by signs in the sky reading "Turn or Burn," but through ordinary people who are redeemed, who display His holiness and proclaim His message of salvation. One of the most winsome and attractive platforms for the saving message is the godly family. He saved us and left us here to rescue the perishing.

The second reason why isolationism does not work as a guard against corruption is for the simple reason that no amount of seclusion will quarantine us from the evil of this age - especially in today's electronic, mobile, consumer context. We live in a fallen world! What's more, even if you could isolate your family in a remote sylvan forest, you still would not be able to get away from yourselves, and you and I my friends are confirmed, certified sinners.

In fact, isolation is one of the worst things a Christian family could ever seek. Isolationism does not encourage godliness at all, rather it breeds suspicion of others - believers as well as the lost – and a judgmental spirit that springs from self-righteous pride.

Concluding Thoughts

If you are reading this book chances are you are alive – I can't imagine this volume being good for much beyond the grave. If this is your lot and you have a family (whether you are at the beginning, middle, or finish line of parenting, and even if you've started the glorious season of grandparenting), understand that your family is under siege.

Your clan of souls is precious to God and plays an important role in His sovereign plan for the ages. Be aware of the battle zones and weaponry you face, and lead your familial flock in the glorious provision the Lord has abundantly supplied for your welfare.

The war on the family will only grow in intensity as our world slips further and further into this post-Christian era. Our response, however, ought always to be the same. We (parents, grandparents) must equip ourselves for godliness by filling our minds and hearts with God's all-sufficient word. In scripture we find the wellspring of truth that leads to a joyous, intimate relationship with the God of our salvation, as well as the sure and tested paths for godly living.

Regardless of the state or rate of social decay surrounding us, it is a thirst for the truth, a love for God, and an obedient life that will preserve us and enable us to shepherd our families. What's more, it is a marriage of truth, a vibrant relationship with our Lord, and an exemplary life that will impact our sons and daughters for Christ and for eternity. This is exactly the course to which God has called His people from ancient times and to the present day.

Look for Marcelo's book "God's Passion and Provision for Your Family." The forthcoming volume will develop the theme of God's provision for your family, pre-release February of 2009.

Introduction To The Duties of Parents

A wise veteran missionary once told me to read three old books for every new one I perused. I believe that's pretty sound advice! I haven't always stuck to that principle (I'm a painfully slow reader!), but I have found that faithful preachers and teachers from bygone eras have unfolded the beauty of Christ and the sweetness of the Bible to me more than modern authors.

Interestingly, the contemporary expositors I'm drawn to today sound a lot like the old guys. Perhaps they have discovered the secret of simply getting in line behind faithful men, who themselves have learned from other faithful men (2 Timothy 2:2). This beats having to cleverly reinvent the ministry wheel with each new generation only to discover in the end you have recreated the cinder block cube – hard to move things forward on a heavy block.

One of the men whose godly influence has risen from the past to bless my life is Pastor J. C. Ryle, an Anglican priest who loved the Lord Jesus and faithfully fed his sheep from the lush green pastures of the word of God. His body of work survives, and indeed flourishes to the great benefit of countless Christians.

Hidden among the treasures left to us by this gentle shepherd is a little known gem by the title of, "The Duties of Parents." It is replete with timeless wisdom for moms and dads who desire to bring their children up in the fear and admonition of the Lord. I have included it in this present volume because I know it will result in your being equipped to shepherd your children (and, or grandchildren) in the tried and true paths of God's truth.

As far as the expert advice I received from a wise missionary, I would encourage you to follow it. Read my book, but read and re-read "The Duties of Parents"!

John Charles Ryle
1816–1900

The Duties of Parents
J. C. Ryle

"Train up a child in the way he should go; even when he is old, he will not depart from it."

Proverbs 22:6

I suppose that most professing Christians are acquainted with the text at the head of this page. The sound of it is probably familiar to your ears, like an old tune. It is likely you have heard it, or read it, talked of it, or quoted it, many a time. Is it not so?

But, after all, how little is the substance of this text regarded! The doctrine it contains appears scarcely known, the duty it puts before us seems fearfully seldom practiced. Reader, do I not speak the truth? It cannot be said that the subject is a new one. The world is old, and we have the experience of nearly six thousand years to help us. We live in days when there is a mighty zeal for education in every quarter. We hear of new schools rising on all sides. We are told of new systems, and new books for the young, of every sort and description. And still for all this, the vast majority of children are manifestly not trained in the way they should go, for when they grow up to man's estate, they do not walk with God. Now how shall we account for this state of things? The plain truth is, the Lord's commandment in our text is not regarded; and therefore the Lord's promise in our text is not fulfilled.

Reader, these things may well give rise to great searchings of heart. Suffer then a word of exhortation from a minister, about the right training of children. Believe me, the subject is one that should come home to every conscience, and make everyone ask himself the question, "Am I in this matter doing what I can?"

It is a subject that concerns almost all. There is hardly a household that it does not touch. Parents, nurses, teachers, grandfathers, grandmothers, uncles, aunts, brothers, and sisters, all have an interest in it. Few can be found, I think, who might not influence some parent in the management of his family, or affect the training of some child by suggestion or advice. All of us, I suspect, can do something here, either directly or indirectly, and I wish to stir up all to bear this in remembrance.

It is a subject, too, on which all concerned are in great danger of coming short of their duty. This is preeminently a point in which men can see the faults of their neighbors more clearly than their own. They will often bring up their children in the very path which they have denounced to their friends as unsafe. They will see motes in other men's families, and overlook beams in their own. They will be quick sighted as eagles in detecting mistakes abroad, and yet blind as bats to fatal errors which are daily going on at home. They will be wise about their brother's house, but foolish about their own flesh and blood. Here, if anywhere, we have need to suspect our own judgment. This, too, you will do well to bear in mind.[1]

Come now, and let me place before you a few hints about right training. God the Father, God the Son, God the Holy Spirit bless them, and make them words in season to you all. Do not reject them because they are blunt and simple; do not despise them because they contain nothing new. Be very sure, if you would train children for heaven, they are hints that ought not to be lightly set aside.

1. If you would train your children rightly, train them in the way they should go, and not in the way that they would.

Remember children are born with a decided bias towards evil, and therefore if you let them choose for themselves, they are certain to choose wrong. The mother cannot tell what her tender infant may grow up to be, tall or short, weak or strong, wise or foolish. He may be any of these things or not; it is all uncertain. But one thing the mother can say with certainty: he will have a corrupt and sinful heart. It comes naturally to us to do wrong. "Folly," says Solomon, "is bound in the heart of a child" (Proverbs 22:15). "A child left to himself brings shame to his mother" (Proverbs 29:15).

Our hearts are like the earth on which we tread; let it alone, and it is sure to bear weeds. If, then, you would deal wisely with your child, you must not leave him to the guidance of his own will. Think for him, judge for him, act for him, just as you would for one weak and blind; but for pity's sake, give him not up to his own wayward tastes and inclinations. It must not be his likings and wishes that are consulted. He knows not yet what is good for his mind and soul, any more than what is good for his body. You do not let him decide what he shall eat, and what he shall drink, and how he shall be clothed. Be consistent, and deal with his mind in like manner. Train him in the way that is scriptural and right, and not in the way that he fancies.

If you cannot make up your mind to this first principle of Christian training, it is useless for you to read any further. Self-will is almost the first thing that appears in a child's mind; and it must be your first step to resist it.

2. *Train up your child with all tenderness, affection, and patience.*

I do not mean that you are to spoil him, but I do mean that you should let him see that you love him.

Love should be the silver thread that runs through all your conduct. Kindness, gentleness, long-suffering, forbearance, patience, sympathy, a willingness to enter into childish troubles, a readiness to take part in childish joys, these are the cords by which a child may be led most easily, these are the clues you must follow if you would find the way to his heart. Few are to be found, even among grown-up people, who are not more easy to draw than to drive. There is that in all our minds which rises in arms against compulsion; we set up our backs and stiffen our necks at the very idea of a forced obedience. We are like young horses in the hand of a breaker: handle them kindly, and make much of them, and by and by you may guide them with thread; use them roughly and violently, and it will be many a month before you get the mastery of them at all.

Now children's minds are cast in much the same mold as our own. Sternness and severity of manner chill them and throw them back. It shuts up their hearts, and you will weary yourself to find the door. But let them only see that you have an affectionate feeling towards them, that you are really desirous to make them happy, and do them good, that if you punish them, it is intended for their profit; let them see this, I say, and they will soon be all your own. But they must be wooed with kindness, if their attention is ever to be won. And surely reason itself might teach us this lesson. Children are weak and tender creatures, and, as such, they need patient and considerate treatment. We must handle them delicately, like frail vessels, lest by rough fingering we do more harm than good. They are like young plants, and need gentle watering, often, but little at a time.

We must not expect all things at once. We must remember what children are, and teach them as they are able to bear. Their minds are like a lump of metal not to be forged and made useful at once, but only by a succession of little blows. Their understandings are like narrow-necked vessels: we must pour in the wine of knowledge gradually, or much of it will be spilled and lost. The whetstone[2] does its work slowly, but frequent rubbing will bring the scythe to a fine edge. Truly there is need of patience in training a child, but without it nothing can be done.

Nothing will compensate for the absence of this tenderness and love. A minister may speak the truth as it is in Jesus, clearly, forcibly, unanswerably; but if he does not speak it in love, few souls will be won. Just so, you must set before your children their duty - command, threaten, punish, reason - but if affection be wanting in your treatment, your labor will be all in vain.

Love is one grand secret of successful training. Anger and harshness may frighten, but they will not persuade the child that you are right; and if he sees you often out of temper, you will soon cease to have his respect. A father who speaks to his son as Saul did to Jonathan (1 Samuel 20:30), need not expect to retain his influence over that son's mind.

Try hard to keep a hold on your child's affections. It is a dangerous thing to make your children afraid of you. Anything is almost better than apprehension and reticence from your child; and this will come in with fear. Fear puts an end to openness of manner; fear leads to concealment; fear sows the seed of much hypocrisy, and leads to many a lie. There is a mine of truth in the Apostle's words to the Colossians: "Fathers, do not provoke your children, lest they be discouraged" (Colossians 3:21). Let not the advice it contains be overlooked.

3. *Train your children with an abiding persuasion on your mind that much depends upon you.*

Grace is the strongest of all principles. See what a revolution grace effects when it comes into the heart of an old sinner, how it overturns the strongholds of Satan, how it casts down mountains, fills up valleys, makes crooked things straight, and new creates the whole man. Truly nothing is impossible to grace. The flesh, too, is very strong. See how it struggles against the things of the kingdom of God, how it fights against every attempt to be more holy, how it keeps up an unceasing warfare within us to the last hour of life. The flesh indeed is strong.

But after the flesh and grace, undoubtedly, there is nothing more powerful than education. Early habits (if I may so speak) are everything with us, under God. We are made what we are by training. Our character takes the form of that mold into which our first years are cast.[3]

We depend, in a vast measure, on those who bring us up. We get from them a color, a taste, a bias which cling to us more or less all our lives. We catch the language of our nurses and mothers, and learn to speak it almost insensibly, and unquestionably we catch something of their manners, ways, and mind at the same time. Time only will show, I suspect, how much we all owe to early impressions, and how many things in us may be traced up to seeds sown in the days of our very infancy, by those who were about us. A very learned Englishman, Mr. Locke, has gone so far as to say: "That of all the men we meet with, nine parts out of ten are what they are, good or bad, useful or not, according to their education."

And all this is one of God's merciful arrangements. He gives your children a mind that will receive impressions like moist clay. He gives them a disposition at the starting-point of life to believe what you tell them, and to accept what you advise them, and to trust your word rather than a stranger's. He gives you, in short, a golden opportunity of doing them good. See that the opportunity not be neglected and thrown away. Once let slip, it is gone forever.

Beware of that miserable delusion into which some have fallen, that parents can do nothing for their children, that you must leave them alone, wait for grace, and sit still. These persons have wishes for their children in Balaam's fashion: they would like them to die the death of the righteous man, but they do nothing to make them live his life. They desire much, and have nothing. And the devil rejoices to see such reasoning, just as he always does over anything which seems to excuse indolence, or to encourage neglect of means.

I know that you cannot convert your child. I know well that they who are born again are born, not of the will of man, but of God (John 1:12-13). But I know also that God says expressly, "Train up a child in the way he should go" (Proverbs 22:6) and that He never laid a command on man which He would not give man grace to perform. And I know, too, that our duty is not to stand still and dispute, but to go forward and obey.

It is just in the going forward that God will meet us. The path of obedience is the way in which He gives the blessing. We have only to do as the servants were commanded at the marriage feast in Cana, to fill the water-pots with water, and we may safely leave it to the Lord to turn that water into wine (John 2:6-10).

4. *Train with this thought continually before your eyes that the soul of your child is the first thing to be considered.*

Precious, no doubt, are these little ones in your eyes; but if you love them, think often of their souls. No interest should weigh with you so much as their eternal interests. No part of them should be so dear to you as that part which will never die. The world, with all its glory, shall pass away; the hills shall melt; the heavens shall be wrapped together as a scroll; the sun shall cease to shine. But the Spirit which dwells in those little creatures, whom you love so well, shall outlive them all, and whether in happiness or misery (to speak as a man) will depend on you.

This is the thought that should be uppermost on your mind in all you do for your children. In every step you take about them, in every plan, and scheme, and arrangement that concerns them, do not leave out that mighty question, "How will this affect their souls?"

Soul love is the soul of all love. To pet and pamper and indulge your child, as if this world was all he had to look to, and this life the only season for happiness - to do this is not true love, but cruelty. It is treating him like some beast of the earth, which has but one world to look to, and nothing after death. It is hiding from him that grand truth, which he ought to be made to learn from his very infancy, that the chief end of his life is the salvation of his soul.

A true Christian must be no slave to convention, if he would train his child for heaven. He must not be content to do things merely because they are the custom of the world:

- To teach them and instruct them in certain ways, merely because it is the accepted "norm";

- To allow them to read books of a questionable sort, merely because everybody else reads them;

- To let them form habits of a doubtful tendency, merely because they are the habits of the day.

Instead, he must train with an eye to his children's souls. He must not be ashamed to hear his training called singular and strange. What if it is? The time is short; the fashion of this world passes away. He that has trained his children for heaven, rather than for earth, for God, rather than for man, he is the parent that will be called wise at last.

5. Train your child to a knowledge of the Bible.

You cannot make your children love the Bible, I allow. None but the Holy Spirit can give us a heart to delight in the Word. But you can make your children acquainted with the Bible; and be sure they cannot be acquainted with that blessed book too soon, or too well.

A thorough knowledge of the Bible is the foundation of all clear views of Christianity. He that is well-grounded in it will not generally be found a waverer, and carried about by every wind of new doctrine. Any system of training which does not make a knowledge of Scripture the first thing is unsafe and unsound.

You have need to be careful on this point just now, for the devil is abroad, and error abounds. Some are to be found amongst us who give the church the honor due to Jesus Christ. Some are to be found who make the sacraments saviors and passports to eternal life. And some are to be found in like manner who honor a catechism more than the Bible, or fill the minds of their children with miserable little story-books, instead of the Scripture of truth. But if you love your children, let the simple Bible be everything in the training of their souls; and let all other books go down and take the second place. Care not so much for their being mighty in the catechism, as for their being mighty in the scriptures. This is the training, believe me, that God will honor.

The Psalmist says of Him, "You have exalted above all things your name and your word" (Psalm 138:2); and I think that He gives a special blessing to all who try to magnify it among men.

- See that your children read the Bible *reverently*. Train them to look on it, not as the word of men, but as it is in truth, the Word of God, written by the Holy Spirit Himself, all true, all profitable, and able to make us wise unto salvation, through faith which is in Christ Jesus.

- See that they read it *regularly*. Train them to regard it as their soul's daily food, as a thing essential to their soul's daily health. I know well you cannot make this anything more than a form; but there is no telling the amount of sin which a mere form may indirectly restrain.

- See that they *read it all*. You need not shrink from bringing any doctrine before them. You need not fancy that the leading doctrines of Christianity are things which children cannot understand. Children understand far more of the Bible than we are apt to suppose.

Tell them of sin, its guilt, its consequences, its power, its vileness: you will find they can comprehend something of this.

Tell them of the Lord Jesus Christ, and His work for our salvation, the atonement, the cross, the blood, the sacrifice, the intercession: you will discover there is much they can comprehend in these great truths.

Tell them of the work of the Holy Spirit in man's heart, how He changes, and renews, and sanctifies, and purifies: you will soon see they can go along with you in some measure in this. In short, I suspect we have no idea how much a little child can take in of the length and breadth of the glorious gospel. They see far more of these things than we suppose.[4]

Fill their minds with Scripture. Let the Word dwell in them richly. Give them the Bible, the whole Bible, even while they are young.

6. *Train them to a habit of prayer.*

- Prayer is the very life-breath of true Christianity. It is one of the first evidences that a man is born again. "Behold," said the Lord of Saul, in the day he sent Ananias to him, "Behold, he is praying" (Acts 9:11). He had begun to pray, and that was proof enough.

- Prayer was the distinguishing mark of the Lord's people in the day that there began to be a separation between them and the world. "At that time people began to call upon the name of the Lord" (Genesis 4:26).

- Prayer is the peculiarity of all real Christians now. They pray, for they tell God their wants, their feelings, their desires, their fears; and mean what they say. The nominal Christian may repeat prayers, and good prayers too, but he goes no further.

- Prayer is the turning-point in a man's soul. Our ministry is unprofitable, and our labor is vain, till you are brought to your knees. Until then, there is no hope for you.

- Prayer is one great secret of spiritual prosperity. When there is much private communion with God, your soul will grow like the grass after rain; when there is little, all will be at a standstill, you will barely keep your soul alive. Show me a growing Christian, a going forward Christian, a strong Christian, a flourishing Christian, and I am sure, he is one that speaks often with his Lord. He asks much, and he has much. He tells Jesus everything, and so he always knows how to act.

- Prayer is the mightiest engine God has placed in our hands. It is the best weapon to use in every difficulty, and the surest remedy in every trouble. It is the key that unlocks the treasury of promises, and the hand that draws forth grace and help in time of need. It is the silver trumpet God commands us to sound in all our necessity, and it is the cry He has promised always to attend to, even as a loving mother to the voice of her child.

- Prayer is the simplest means that man can use in coming to God. It is within reach of all - the sick, the aged, the infirm, the paralytic, the blind, the poor, the unlearned - all can pray. It avails you nothing to plead want of memory, and want of learning, and want of books, and want of scholarship in this matter. So long as you have a tongue to tell your soul's state, you may and ought to pray. Those words, "You do not have, because you do not ask" (James. 4:2), will be a fearful condemnation to many in the day of judgment.

Parents, if you love your children, do all that lies in your power to train them up to a habit of prayer. Show them how to begin. Tell them what to say. Encourage them to persevere. Remind them if they become careless and slack about it. Let it not be your fault, at any rate, if they never call on the name of the Lord. This, remember, is the first step in a relationship with God which a child is able to take.

Long before he can read, you can teach him to kneel by his mother's side, and repeat the simple words of prayer and praise which she puts in his mouth. And as the first steps in any undertaking are always the most important, so is the manner in which your children's prayers are prayed, a point which deserves your closest attention. Few seem to know how much depends on this. You must beware lest they get into a way of saying them in a hasty, careless, and irreverent manner.

You must beware of giving up the oversight of this matter to others (Christian professionals: youth pastors, children's workers, et. al.), or of trusting too much to your children doing it when left to themselves. I cannot praise that mother who never looks after this most important part of her child's daily life herself. Surely if there be any habit which your own hand and eye should help in forming, it is the habit of prayer.

Believe me, if you never hear your children pray yourself, you are much to blame. You are little wiser than the bird described in Job, "For she leaves her eggs to the earth and lets them be warmed on the ground, forgetting that a foot may crush them and that the wild beast may trample them. She deals cruelly with her young, as if they were not hers; though her labor be in vain, yet she has no fear" (Job 39:14-16).

Prayer is, of all habits, the one which we recollect the longest. Many a grey-headed man could tell you how his mother used to make him pray in the days of his childhood. Other things have passed away from his mind perhaps. The church where he was taken to worship, the minister whom he heard preach, the companions who used to play with him - all these, it may be, have passed from his memory, and left no mark behind. But you will often find it is far different with his first prayers. He will often be able to tell you where he knelt, and what he was taught to say, and even how his mother looked all the while. It will come up as fresh before his mind's eye as if it was but yesterday.

Reader, if you love your children, I charge you, do not let the seed-time of a prayerful habit pass away unimproved. If you train your children to anything, train them, at least, to a habit of prayer.

7. *Train them to habits of diligence, and regularity about public means of grace.*[5]

- Tell them of the duty and privilege of going to church, and joining in the prayers of the congregation.

- Tell them that wherever the Lord's people are gathered together, there the Lord Jesus is present in a special manner, and that those who absent themselves must expect, like the Apostle Thomas, to miss a blessing.

- Tell them of the importance of hearing the Word preached, and that it is God's ordinance for converting, sanctifying, and building up the souls of men.

- Tell them how Scripture enjoins us, "not neglecting to meet together, as is the habit of some" (Hebrews 10:25); but to exhort one another, to stir one another up to it, and so much the more as we see the day approaching.[6]

I call it a sad sight in a church when nobody comes up to the Lord's table but the elderly people, and the young men and the young women all turn away. But I call it a sadder sight still when no children are to be seen in a church, excepting those who come to the Sunday School, and are obliged to attend. Let none of this guilt lie at your doors. There are many boys and girls in every parish, besides those who come to school, and you who are their parents and friends should see to it that they come with you to church.

Do not allow them to grow up with a habit of making vain excuses for not coming. Give them plainly to understand, that so long as they are under your roof it is the rule of your house for every one in health to honor worship on the Lord's day, and that you reckon he who doesn't, to be a murderer of his own soul.

See to it too, if it can be so arranged, that your children go with you to church, and sit near you when they are there. To go to church is one thing, but to behave well at church is quite another. And believe me, there is no security for good behavior like that of having them under your own eye.

The minds of young people are easily drawn aside, and their attention lost, and every possible means should be used to counteract this. Neither do I like to see what I call "a young people's corner" in a church. They often catch habits of inattention and irreverence there, which it takes years to unlearn, if ever they are unlearned at all. What I like to see is a whole family sitting together, old and young, side by side - men, women, and children, serving God according to their households.

But there are some who say that it is useless to urge children to attend means of grace, because they cannot understand them. I would not have you listen to such reasoning. I find no such doctrine in the Old Testament. When Moses goes before Pharaoh, I observe he says, "We will go with our young and our old. We will go with our sons and daughters... for we must hold a feast to the LORD" (Exodus 10:9). When Joshua read the law, I observe, "There was not a word of all that Moses commanded that Joshua did not read before all the assembly of Israel, and the women, and the little ones, and the sojourners who lived among them" (Joshua 8:35). "Three times in the year," says Exodus 34:23, "shall all your males appear before the LORD God, the God of Israel."

And when I turn to the New Testament, I find children mentioned there as partaking in public acts of worship as well as in the Old. When Paul was leaving the disciples at Tyre for the last time, I find it said, "They all, with wives and children, accompanied us until we were out of the city. And kneeling down on the beach, we prayed" (Acts 21:5).

Parents, comfort your minds with these examples. Do not be discouraged that your children do not see the full value of the means of grace now. Only train them up to a habit of consistent worship. Set it before their minds as a high, holy, and solemn duty, and believe me, the day will very likely come when they will bless you for your deed.

8. Train them to a habit of trust.

I mean by this, you should train them up to believe what you say. You should try to make them feel confidence in your judgment, and respect your opinions, as better than their own. You should accustom them to think that, when you say a thing is bad for them, it must be bad, and when you say it is good for them, it must be good; that your knowledge, in short, is better than their own, and that they may rely implicitly on your word. Teach them to feel that what they do not know now, they will probably know hereafter, and to be satisfied there is a reason for everything you require them to do.

Who indeed can describe the blessedness of a real spirit of faith? Or rather, who can tell the misery that unbelief has brought upon the world? Unbelief made Eve eat the forbidden fruit; she doubted the truth of God's word: "You shall surely die" (Genesis 2:17). Unbelief made the old world reject Noah's warning, and so perish in sin.

Unbelief kept Israel in the wilderness; it was the bar that kept them from entering the promised land. Unbelief made the Jews crucify the Lord of glory; they did not believe the voice of Moses and the prophets, though read to them everyday. And unbelief is the reigning sin of man's heart down to this very hour: unbelief in God's promises, unbelief in God's admonitions, unbelief in our own sinfulness, unbelief in our own danger, unbelief in everything that runs counter to the pride and worldliness of our evil hearts. Reader, you train your children to little purpose if you do not train them to a habit of implicit trust, trust in their parents' word, confidence that what their parents say must be right.

I have heard it said by some, that you should require nothing of children which they cannot understand, that you should explain and give a reason for everything you desire them to do. I warn you solemnly against such a notion. I tell you plainly, I think it an unsound and rotten principle. No doubt it is absurd to make a mystery of everything you do, and there are many things which it is well to explain to children, in order that they may see that they are reasonable and wise.

But to bring them up with the idea that they must take nothing on trust, that they, with their weak and imperfect understandings, must have the "why" and the "wherefore" made clear to them at every step they take, this is indeed a fearful mistake, and likely to have the worst effect on their minds.

Reason with your child if you are so disposed, at certain times, but never forget to keep him in mind (if you really love him) that he is but a child after all - that he thinks as a child, he understands as a child, and therefore must not expect to know the reason of everything at once.

Set before him the example of Isaac, in the day when Abraham took him to offer him on Mount Moriah (Genesis 22). He asked his father that single question, "Where is the lamb for a burnt-offering?" and he got no answer but this, "God will provide for himself the lamb." How, or where, or whence, or in what manner, or by what means - all this Isaac was not told, but the answer was enough. He believed that it would be well, because his father said so, and he was content. Tell your children, too, that we must all be learners in our beginnings, that there is an alphabet to be mastered in every kind of knowledge, that the best horse in the world had need once to be broken, that a day will come when they will see the wisdom of all your training. But in the meantime if you say a thing is right, it must be enough for them; they must believe you, and be content.

Parents, if any point in training is important, it is this. I charge you by the affection you have for your children, use every means to train them up to a habit of faith.

9. Train them to a habit of obedience.

This is an object which it is worth any labor to attain. No habit, I suspect, has such an influence over our lives as this. Parents, determine to make your children obey you, though it may cost you much trouble, and cost them many tears. Let there be no questioning, and reasoning, and disputing, and delaying, and answering again. When you give them a command, let them see plainly that you will have it done.

Obedience is the only reality. It is faith visible, faith acting, and faith incarnate. It is the test of real discipleship among the Lord's people. "You are my friends if you do what I command you" (John 15:14). It ought to be the mark of well-trained children, that they do whatsoever their parents command them. Where, in deed, is the honor which the fifth commandment enjoins, if fathers and mothers are not obeyed cheerfully, willingly, and at once?[7]

Early obedience has all Scripture on its side. It is to Abraham's praise, that he not only trained his family, but that he would "command his children and his household after him" (Genesis 18:19). It is said of the Lord Jesus Christ Himself, that when He was young He was subject to Mary and Joseph" (Luke 2:51).

Observe how implicitly Joseph obeyed the order of his father Jacob (Genesis 37:13). See how Isaiah speaks of it as an evil thing, when "the youth will be insolent to the elder" (Isaiah 3:5). Mark how the Apostle Paul names disobedience to parents as one of the bad signs of the latter days (2 Timothy 3:2). Mark how he singles out this grace of requiring obedience as one that should adorn a Christian minister: "He (an overseer, i.e. an elder) must manage his own household well, with all dignity keeping his children submissive." And again, let deacons manage "their children and their own households well" (1 Timothy 3:4,12). And again, an elder must be one whose "children are believers and not open to the charge of debauchery or insubordination" (Titus 1:6).

Parents, do you wish to see your children happy? Take care, then, that you train them to obey when they are spoken to, to do as they are bid. Believe me, we are not made for entire independence; we are not fit for it. Even Christ's freemen have a yoke to wear, they "are serving the Lord Christ" (Colossians 3:24). Children cannot learn too soon that this is a world in which we are not all intended to rule, and that we are never in our right place until we know how to obey our betters. Teach them to obey while young, or else they will be fretting against God all their lives long, and wear themselves out with the vain idea of being independent of His control.

Reader, this hint is only too much needed. You will see many in this day who allow their children to choose and think for themselves long before they are able, and even make excuses for their disobedience, as if it were a thing not to be blamed. To my eyes, a parent always yielding, and a child always having its own way, are a most painful sight - painful, because I see God's appointed order of things inverted and turned upside down - painful, because I feel sure the consequence to that child's character in the end will be self-will, pride, and self-conceit. You must not wonder that men refuse to obey their Father which is in heaven, if you allow them, when children, to disobey their father who is upon earth.

Parents, if you love your children, let obedience be a motto and a watchword continually before their eyes.

10. *Train them to a habit of always speaking the truth.*

Truth-speaking is far less common in the world than we are prone to think. The whole truth, and nothing but the truth, is a golden rule which many would do well to bear in mind. Lying and prevarication are old sins. The devil was the father of them; he deceived Eve by a bold lie, and ever since the fall it is a sin against which all the children of Eve have need to be on their guard.

Only think how much falsehood and deceit there is in the world! How much exaggeration! How many additions are made to a simple story! How many things left out, if it does not serve the speaker's interest to tell them! How few there are about us of whom we can say, we put unhesitating trust in their word!

Truly the ancient Persians were wise in their generation: it was a leading point with them in educating their children that they should learn to speak the truth. What an awful proof it is of man's natural sinfulness, that it should be needful to name such a point at all!

Reader, I would have you remark how often God is spoken of in the Old Testament as the God of truth. Truth seems to be especially set before us as a leading feature in the character of Him with whom we have to do. He never swerves from the straight line. He abhors lying and hypocrisy.

Try to keep this continually before your children's minds. Press upon them at all times, that less than the truth is a lie; that evasion, excuse-making, and exaggeration are all halfway houses towards what is false, and ought to be avoided. Encourage them in any circumstances to be straightforward, and, whatever it may cost them, to speak the truth.

I press this subject on your attention, not merely for the sake of your children's character in the world - though I might dwell much on this - I urge it rather for your own comfort and assistance in all your dealings with them. You will find it a mighty help indeed, to be able always to trust their word. It will go far to prevent that habit of concealment, which so unhappily prevails sometimes among children. Openness and straightforwardness depend much upon a parent's treatment of this matter in the days of childhood.

11. *Train them to a habit of always redeeming the time.*

Idleness is the devil's best friend. It is the surest way to give him an opportunity of doing us harm. An idle mind is like an open door, and if Satan does not enter in himself by it, it is certain he will throw in something to raise bad thoughts in our souls.

No created being was ever meant to be idle. Service and work is the appointed portion of every creature of God. The angels in heaven work; they are the Lord's ministering servants, ever doing His will. Adam, in Paradise, had work; he was appointed to dress the garden of Eden, and to keep it. The redeemed saints in glory will have work, "They rest not day and night singing praise and glory to Him who bought them." And man, weak, sinful man, must have something to do, or else his soul will soon get into an unhealthy state. We must have our hands filled, and our minds occupied with something, or else our imaginations will soon ferment and breed mischief.

And what is true of us, is true of our children too. Alas, indeed, for the man that has nothing to do! The Jews thought idleness a positive sin: it was a law of theirs that every man should bring up his son to some useful trade, and they were right. They knew the heart of man better than some of us appear to do.

Idleness made Sodom what she was. "Behold, this was the guilt of your sister Sodom: she and her daughters had pride, excess of food, and prosperous ease" (Ezekiel 16:49). Idleness had much to do with David's awful sin with the wife of Uriah. I see in 2 Samuel 11 that Joab went out to war against Ammon, "But David remained at Jerusalem." Was not that idle? And then it was that he saw Bathsheba, and the next step we read of is his tremendous and miserable fall.

Truly, I believe that idleness has led to more sin than almost any other habit that could be named. I suspect it is the mother of many a work of the flesh - the mother of adultery, fornication, drunkenness, and many other deeds of darkness that I have not time to name. Let your own conscience say whether I do not speak the truth. You were idle, and at once the devil knocked at the door and came in.

And indeed I do not wonder; everything in the world around us seems to teach the same lesson. It is the still water which becomes stagnant and impure: the running, moving streams are always clear. If you have steam machinery, you must work it, or it soon gets out of order. If you have a horse, you must exercise him; he is never so well as when he has regular work.

If you would have good bodily health yourself, you must take exercise. If you always sit still, your body is sure at length to complain. And just so is it with the soul. The active moving mind is a hard mark for the devil to shoot at. Try to be always full of useful employment, and thus your enemy will find it difficult to get room to sow tares.

Reader, I ask you to set these things before the minds of your children. Teach them the value of time, and try to make them learn the habit of using it well. It pains me to see children idling over what they have in hand, whatever it may be.

I love to see them active and industrious, and giving their whole heart to all they do; giving their whole heart to lessons, when they have to learn; giving their whole heart even to their amusements, when they go to play.

But if you love them well, let idleness be counted a sin in your family.

12. Train them with a constant fear of over-indulgence.

This is the one point of all on which you have most need to be on your guard. It is natural to be tender and affectionate towards your own flesh and blood, and it is the excess of this very tenderness and affection which you have to fear. Take heed that it does not make you blind to your children's faults, and deaf to all advice about them. Take heed lest it make you overlook bad conduct, rather than have the pain of inflicting punishment and correction.

I know well that punishment and correction are disagreeable things. Nothing is more unpleasant than giving pain to those we love, and calling forth their tears. But so long as hearts are what hearts are, it is vain to suppose, as a general rule, that children can ever be brought up without correction.

Spoiling is a very expressive word, and sadly full of meaning. Now it is the shortest way to spoil children to let them have their own way, to allow them to do wrong and not to punish them for it. Believe me, you must not do it, whatever pain it may cost you unless you wish to ruin your children's souls.

You cannot say that Scripture does not speak expressly on this subject:

- "Whoever spares the rod, hates his son; but he who loves him is diligent to discipline him" (Proverbs 13:24).

- "Discipline your son, for there is hope; do not set your heart on putting him to death" (Proverbs 19:18).

- "Folly is bound in the heart of a child, but the rod of discipline drives it far from him" (Proverbs 22:15).

- "Do not withhold discipline from a child; if you strike him with a rod, he will not die. If you strike him with the rod, you will save his soul from Sheol" (Proverbs 23:13,14).

- "The rod and reproof give wisdom, but a child left to himself brings shame to his mother." "Discipline your son, and he will give you rest, he will give delight to your soul" (Proverbs 29:15,17).

How strong and forcible are these texts! How melancholy is the fact, that in many Christian families they seem almost unknown! Their children need reproof, but it is hardly ever given; they need correction, but it is hardly ever employed. And yet this book of Proverbs is not obsolete and unfit for Christians. It is given by inspiration of God, and profitable. It is given for our learning, even as the Epistles to the Romans and Ephesians. Surely the believer who brings up his children without attention to its counsel is making himself wise above that which is written, and greatly errs.

Fathers and mothers, I tell you plainly, if you never punish your children when they are in fault, you are doing them a grievous wrong. I warn you, this is the rock on which the saints of God, in every age, have only too frequently made shipwreck. I would fain persuade you to be wise in time, and keep clear of it.

See it in Eli's case. His sons Hophni and Phinehas "were blaspheming God, and he did not restrain them." He gave them no more than a tame and lukewarm reproof, when he ought to have rebuked them sharply. In one word, he honored his sons above God. And what was the end of these things? He lived to hear of the death of both his sons in battle, and his own grey hairs were brought down with sorrow to the grave (1 Samuel 2:22-29, 3:13).

See, too, the case of David. Who can read without pain the history of his children, and their sins? Ammon's incest, Absalom's murder and proud rebellion, Adonijah's scheming ambition: truly these were grievous wounds for the man after God's own heart to receive from his own house. But was there no fault on his side? I fear there can be no doubt there was. I find a clue to it all in the account of Adonijah in 1 Kings 1:6, "His father had never at any time displeased him by asking, 'Why have you done thus and so?'" There was the foundation of all the mischief. David was an over-indulgent father, a father who let his children have their own way, and he reaped according as he had sown.

Parents, I beseech you, for your children's sake, beware of over-indulgence. I call on you to remember, it is your first duty to consult their real interests, and not their fancies and likings: to train them, not to humor them - to profit, not merely to please.

You must not give way to every wish and caprice of your child's mind, however much you may love him. You must not let him suppose his will is to be everything, and that he has only to desire a thing and it will be done. Do not, I pray you, make your children idols, lest God should take them away, and break your idol, just to convince you of your folly.

Learn to say "No" to your children. Show them that you are able to refuse whatever you think is not fit for them. Show them that you are ready to punish disobedience, and that when you speak of punishment, you are not only ready to threaten, but also to perform. Do not threaten too much.[8] Threatened folks, and threatened faults, live long. Punish seldom, but really and in good earnest, frequent and slight punishment is a wretched system indeed.[9]

Beware of letting small faults pass unnoticed under the idea "it is a little one." There are no little things in training children; all are important. Little weeds need plucking up as much as any. Leave them alone, and they will soon be great. Reader, if there be any point which deserves your attention, believe me, it is this one. It is one that will give you trouble, I know. But if you do not take trouble with your children when they are young, they will give you trouble when they are old. Choose which you prefer.

13. *Train them remembering continually how God trains His children.*

The Bible tells us that God has an elect people, a family in this world. All poor sinners who have been convinced of sin, and fled to Jesus for peace, make up that family. All of us who really believe on Christ for salvation are its members. Now God the Father is ever training the members of this family for their everlasting abode with Him in heaven. He acts as a husbandman pruning his vines, that they may bear more fruit. He knows the character of each of us: our besetting sins, our weaknesses, our peculiar infirmities, our special wants. He knows our works and where we dwell, who are our companions in life, and what are our trials, what our temptations, and what are our privileges.

He knows all these things, and is ever ordering all for our good. He allots to each of us, in His providence, the very things we need, in order to bear the most fruit, as much of sunshine as we can stand, and as much of rain, as much of bitter things as we can bear, and as much of sweet. Reader, if you would train your children wisely, mark well how God the Father trains His. He does all things well; the plan which He adopts must be right.

See, then, how many things there are which God withholds from His children. Few could be found, I suspect, among them who have not had desires which He has never been pleased to fulfill. There has often been some one thing they wanted to attain, and yet there has always been some barrier to prevent attainment. It has been just as if God was placing it above our reach, and saying, "This is not good for you; this must not be." Moses desired exceedingly to cross over Jordan, and see the goodly land of promise; but you will remember his desire was never granted.

See, too, how often God leads His people by ways which seem dark and mysterious to our eyes. We cannot see the meaning of all His dealings with us; we cannot see the reasonableness of the path in which our feet are treading.

Sometimes so many trials have assailed us, so many difficulties encompassed us, that we have not been able to discover the purpose of it all. It has been just as if our Father was taking us by the hand into a dark place and saying, "Ask no questions, but follow Me." There was a direct road from Egypt to Canaan, yet Israel was not led into it; but round, through the wilderness. And this seemed hard at the time. "And the people," we are told, "became impatient on the way" (Exodus 13:17; Numbers 21:4).

See, also, how often God chastens His people with trial and affliction. He sends them crosses and disappointments; He lays them low with sickness; He strips them of property and friends; He changes them from one position to another; He visits them with things most hard to flesh and blood; and some of us have well-nigh fainted under the burdens laid upon us. We have felt pressed beyond strength, and have been almost ready to murmur at the hand which chastened us. Paul the Apostle had a thorn in the flesh appointed him, some bitter bodily trial, no doubt, though we know not exactly what it was. But this we know, he implored the Lord three times that it might be removed; yet it was not taken away (2 Corinthians 12:8, 9).

Now, reader, notwithstanding all these things, did you ever hear of a single child of God who thought his Father did not treat him wisely? No, I am sure you never did. God's children would always tell you, in the long run, it was a blessed thing they did not have their own way, and that God had done far better for them than they could have done for themselves. Yes! And they could tell you, too, that God's dealings had provided more happiness for them than they ever would have obtained themselves, and that His way, however dark at times, was the way of pleasantness and the path of peace.

I ask you to lay to heart the lesson which God's dealings with His people is meant to teach you. Do not fear to withhold from your child anything you think will do him harm, whatever his own wishes may be. This is God's plan. Do not hesitate to lay on him commands, of which he may not at present see the wisdom, and to guide him in ways which may not now seem reasonable to his mind. This is God's plan.

Do not shrink from chastening and correcting him whenever you see his soul's health requires it, however painful it may be to your feelings; and remember medicines for the mind must not be rejected because they are bitter. This is God's plan.

And do not be afraid, above all, that such a plan of training will make your child unhappy. I warn you against this delusion. Depend on it, there is no surer road to unhappiness than always having our own way. To have our wills checked and denied is a blessed thing for us; it makes us value enjoyments when they come. To be indulged perpetually is the way to be made selfish; and selfish people and spoiled children, believe me, are seldom happy.

Reader, do not be wiser than God; train your children as He trains His.

14. *Train them remembering continually the influence of your own example.*

Instruction, and advice, and commands will profit little, unless they are backed up by the pattern of your own life. Your children will never believe you are in earnest, and really wish them to obey you, so long as your actions contradict your counsel. Archbishop Tillotson made a wise remark when he said, "To give children good instruction, and a bad example, is but beckoning to them with the head to show them the way to heaven, while we take them by the hand and lead them in the way to hell."

We little know the force and power of example. No one of us can live to himself in this world; we are always influencing those around us, in one way or another, either for good or for evil, either for God or for sin. They see our ways, they mark our conduct, they observe our behavior, and what they see us practice, that they may fairly suppose we think right. And never, I believe, does example tell so powerfully as it does in the case of parents and children.

Fathers and mothers, do not forget that children learn more by the eye than they do by the ear. No school will make such deep marks on character as home. The best of schoolmasters will not imprint on their minds as much as they will pick up at your fireside. Imitation is a far stronger principle with children than memory. What they see has a much stronger effect on their minds than what they are told.

Take care, then, what you do before a child. It is a true proverb, "Who sins before a child, sins double." Strive rather to be a living epistle of Christ, such as your families can read, and that plainly too. Be an example of reverence for the Word of God, reverence in prayer, reverence for means of grace, reverence for the Lord's day. Be an example in words, in temper, in diligence, in temperance, in faith, in charity, in kindness, in humility. Do not think your children will practice what they do not see you do. You are their model picture, and they will copy what you are. Your reasoning and your lecturing, your wise commands and your good advice; all this they may not understand, but they can understand your life.

Children are very quick observers; very quick in seeing through some kinds of hypocrisy, very quick in finding out what you really think and feel, very quick in adopting all your ways and opinions. You will often find as the father is, so is the son.

Remember the word that the conqueror Caesar always used to his soldiers in a battle. He did not say "Go forward," but "Come." So it must be with you in training your children. They will seldom learn habits which they see you despise, or walk in paths in which you do not walk yourself. He that preaches to his children what he does not practice, is working a work that never goes forward. It is like the fabled web of Penelope of old, who wove all day, and unwove all night. Even so, the parent who tries to train without setting a good example is building with one hand, and pulling down with the other.

15. *Train them remembering continually the power of sin.*

I mention this briefly, in order to guard you against unscriptural expectations. You must not expect to find your children's minds a sheet of pure white paper, and to have no trouble if you only use right means. I warn you plainly you will find no such thing. It is painful to see how much corruption and evil there is in a young child's heart, and how soon it begins to bear fruit. Violent tempers, self-will, pride, envy, sullenness, passion, idleness, selfishness, deceit, cunning, falsehood, hypocrisy, a terrible aptness to learn what is bad, a painful slowness to learn what is good, a readiness to pretend anything in order to gain their own ends, all these things, or some of them, you must be prepared to see, even in your own flesh and blood. In little ways they will creep out at a very early age; it is almost startling to observe how naturally they seem to spring up. Children require no schooling to learn to sin.

But you must not be discouraged and cast down by what you see. You must not think it a strange and unusual thing, that little hearts can be so full of sin. It is the only portion which our father Adam left us; it is that fallen nature with which we come into the world; it is that inheritance which belongs to us all. Let it rather make you more diligent in using every means which seem most likely, by God's blessing, to counteract the mischief. Let it make you more and more careful, so far as in you lies, to keep your children out of the way of temptation.

Never listen to those who tell you your children are good, and well brought up, and can be trusted. Think rather that their hearts are always inflammable as tinder. At their very best, they only want a spark to set their corruptions alight. Parents are seldom too cautious. Remember the natural depravity of your children, and take care.

16. *Train them remembering continually the promises of Scripture.*

I also mention this briefly, in order to guard you against discouragement. You have a plain promise on your side, "Train up a child in the way he should go; even when he is old, he will not depart from it" (Proverbs 22:6). Think what it is to have a promise like this. Promises were the only lamp of hope which cheered the hearts of the patriarchs before the Bible was written. Enoch, Noah, Abraham, Isaac, Jacob, Joseph, all lived on a few promises, and prospered in their souls. Promises are the cordials which in every age have supported and strengthened the believer. He that has got a plain text upon his side need never be cast down. Fathers and mothers, when your hearts are failing, and ready to halt, look at the word of this text, and take comfort.

Think who it is that promises. It is not the word of a man, who may lie or repent; it is the word of the King of kings, who never changes. Has He said a thing, and shall He not do it? Or has He spoken, and shall He not make it good? Neither is anything too hard for Him to perform. The things that are impossible with men are possible with God. Reader, if we do not get the benefit of the promise we are dwelling upon, the fault is not in Him, but in ourselves.

Think, too, what the promise contains, before you refuse to take comfort from it. It speaks of a certain time when good training shall especially bear fruit, "when a child is old." Surely there is comfort in this. You may not see with your own eyes the result of careful training, but you do not know what blessed fruits may spring from it, long after you are dead and gone.

It is not God's way to give everything at once. "Afterwards" is the time when He often chooses to work, both in the things of nature and in the things of grace. "Afterward" is the season when affliction bears the peaceable fruit of righteousness (Hebrews 12:11). "Afterward" was the time when the son who refused to work in his father's vineyard repented and went (Matthew 21:29). And "afterward" is the time to which parents must look forward if they do not see success at once; you must sow in hope and plant in hope.

"Cast your bread upon the waters," says the Spirit, "for you will find it after many days" (Ecclesiastes 11:1). Many children, I do not doubt, shall rise up in the day of judgment, and bless their parents for good training, who never gave any signs of having profited by it during their parents' lives. Go forward then in faith, and be sure that your labor shall not be altogether thrown away. Three times did Elijah stretch himself upon the widow's child before it revived. Take example from him, and persevere.

17. *Train them, lastly, with continual prayer for a blessing on all you do.*

Without the blessing of the Lord, your best endeavors will do no good. He has the hearts of all men in His hands, and except He touch the hearts of your children by His Spirit, you will weary yourself to no purpose. Water, therefore, the seed you sow on their minds with unceasing prayer. The Lord is far more willing to hear than we to pray; far more ready to give blessings than we to ask them; but He loves to be entreated for them. And I set this matter of prayer before you, as the top-stone and seal of all you do. I suspect the child of many prayers is seldom cast away.

Look upon your children as Jacob did on his; he tells Esau they are "the children whom God has graciously given your servant" (Genesis 33:5). Look on them as Joseph did on his; he told his father, "They are my sons, whom God has given me here" (Genesis 48:9). Count them with the Psalmist to be "a heritage from the Lord, the fruit of the womb a reward" (Psalm 127:3). And then ask the Lord, with a holy boldness, to be gracious and merciful to His own gifts.

Mark how Abraham intercedes for Ishmael, because he loved him, "Oh that Ishmael might live before You" (Genesis 17:18). See how Manoah speaks to the angel about Samson, "What is to be the child's manner of life, and what is his mission?" (Judges 13:12). Observe how tenderly Job cared for his children's souls, "And when the days of the feast had run their course, Job would send, and consecrate them, and he would rise early in the morning and offer burnt offerings according to the number of them all. For Job said, "It may be that my children have sinned, and cursed God in their hearts." Thus Job did continually" (Job 1:5). Parents, if you love your children, go and do likewise. You cannot name their names before the mercy-seat too often.

And now, reader, in conclusion, let me once more press upon you the necessity and importance of using every single means in your power, if you would train children for heaven.

I know well that God is a sovereign God, and does all things according to the counsel of His own will. I know that Rehoboam was the son of Solomon, and Manasseh the son of Hezekiah, and that you do not always see godly parents having a godly seed. But I know also that God is a God who works by means, and I am sure, if you make light of such means as I have mentioned, your children are not likely to turn out well.

Fathers and mothers, you may dedicate your children to Christ, and enroll them in the ranks of Christ's church; you may get godly sponsors to answer for them, and help you by their prayers; you may send them to the best of schools, and give them Bibles and Prayer Books, and fill them with head knowledge, but if all this time there is no regular training at home, I tell you plainly, I fear it will go hard in the end with your children's souls.

- Home is the place where habits are formed;

- Home is the place where the foundations of character are laid;

- Home gives the bias to our tastes, and likings, and opinions.

See to it, I beg you, that there be careful training at home. Happy indeed is the man who can say, as Bolton did upon his dying bed, to his children, "I do believe not one of you will dare to meet me before the tribunal of Christ in an unregenerate state."

Fathers and mothers, I charge you solemnly before God and the Lord Jesus Christ, take every pain to train your children in the way they should go. I charge you not merely for the sake of your children's souls; I charge you for the sake of your own future comfort and peace. Truly it is your interest to so do. Truly your own happiness in great measure depends on it. Children have ever been the bow from which the sharpest arrows have pierced man's heart.

Children have mixed the bitterest cups that man has ever had to drink. Children have caused the saddest tears that man has ever had to shed. Adam could tell you so; Jacob could tell you so; David could tell you so. There are no sorrows on earth like those which children have brought upon their parents. Oh! take heed, lest your own neglect should lay up misery for you in your old age. Take heed, lest you weep under the ill-treatment of a thankless child, in the days when your eye is dim, and your natural force abated.

If ever you wish your children to be the restorers of your life, and the nourishers of your old age, if you would have them blessings and not curses - joys and not sorrows - Judahs and not Reubens - Ruths and not Orpahs, if you would not, like Noah, be ashamed of their deeds, and like Rebekah, be made weary of your life by them: if this is your longing, remember my advice often, train them while young in the right way.

And as for me, I will conclude by putting up my prayer to God for all who read this paper, that you may all be taught of God to feel the value of your own souls. This is one reason why baptism is too often a mere form, and Christian training despised and disregarded. Too often parents do not have regard for their own souls, and so they disregard the souls of their children. They do not realize the tremendous difference between a state of nature and a state of grace, and therefore they are content to let them alone.

Now the Lord teach you all, that sin is that abominable thing which God hates. Then, I know you will mourn over the sins of your children, and strive to pluck them out as brands from the fire.

The Lord teach you all how precious Christ is, and what a mighty and complete work He has done for our salvation. Then, I feel confident you will use every means to bring your children to Jesus, that they may live through Him. The Lord teach you all your need of the Holy Spirit, to renew, sanctify, and quicken your souls. Then, I feel sure you will urge your children to pray to Him without ceasing, and never rest till He has come down into their hearts with power, and made them new creatures.

The Lord grant this, and then I have a good hope that you will indeed train up your children well, train well for this life, and train well for the life to come; train well for earth, and train well for heaven; train them for God, for Christ, and for eternity.

Protecting Your Home Endnotes

Chapter 1 Endnotes

1. Allan David Bloom, The Closing of the American Mind (New York, NY: Simon & Schuster, 1987), p. 25.

Chapter 2 Endnotes

1. The best place to start effective Bible study is with an excellent translation such as the New American Standard Bible (NASB), or the New King James Version (NKJV). The English Standard Version of the Bible (ESV) reads well and provides an excellent rendition of the biblical text as well. If you're in the market for a new Bible, make sure you get one with a reference tool in the margins. The small font abbreviations along the edges or in the middle of the page are valuable citations to parallel passages or similar texts in other parts of the Bible.

If you are new to the study of the Bible, three valuable tools for your library would be a good Bible dictionary (Eerdman's Bible Dictionary), a study Bible (The MacArthur Study Bible, in my opinion, is the best study Bible on the market), and an exhaustive concordance (the New American Standard Exhaustive Concordance for the NASB, The New Strong's Exhaustive Concordance for the New King James Version).

2. The paragraph of Colossians 3:12-17 is followed by an exhortation to married couples in verse 18. This passage (v 12-21) would also make a fantastic text to study and appropriate to your home!

3. These two texts (Colossians 3:12-21 and Ephesians 5:15-33) establish an undeniable connection between a life controlled by the Holy Spirit and a godly marriage).

Chapter 3 Endnotes

1. "Last days" is a technical term of the New Testament referring to the time from the cross to the second coming.

Chapter 4 Endnotes

1. The phrase "fear of the Lord" in the Bible is often used to speak of a believer's reverential awe for God. It involves a worshipful reverence for the person of God - all His attributes, particularly His holiness – His marvelous works, His unparalleled revelation, and demonstrated in our response of loving obedience.

2. "mature over time" Parents exercise more control in early childhood and their role increasingly develops into a come-along-side consultant roll in young adulthood.

3. Three of Job's latter sons are named in 42:14. God blessed Job with ten more children after his testing. The events recorded in the book of Job likely took place during the patriarchal period (the days of Abraham, Isaac, and Jacob) when the lifespan of men reached the 150 to 200 year range. This enabled Job and his wife to experience the birth and life of ten additional children, as well as many grandchildren.

4. Keil and Delitzsch, Commentary on the Old Testament, Volume IV, Job, (Grand Rapids, MI, William B. Eerdmans Publishing Company, Reprinted 1975), Pg. 51. Even thought the suffixes in the Hebrew are masculine ("sons") this refers to all ten children. This is a common way in Hebrew to refer to both sons and daughters.

5. R. Laird Harris, Gleason L. Archer, Jr. and Bruce K. Waltke, Theological Wordbook of the Old Testament, Vol. 2, (Chicago, Moody Press, 1980), qadash pp. 786-787.

6. Francis Brown, S.R. Driver, and C.A. Briggs, A Hebrew and English Lexicon of the Old Testament, (Oxford, Clarendon Press, Reprint 1951), Pg. 872-873.

7. R. Laird Harris, Gleason L. Archer, Jr. and Bruce K. Waltke, Theological Wordbook of the Old Testament, Vol. 2, (Chicago, Moody Press, 1980), pp. 585-586.

8. NAS Exhaustive Concordance, ekplesso, literally "to strike" meaning "to strike with panic," Liddell & Scott, "to drive out of one's senses." Both references from Accordance Bible Software, (Altamonte Springs, FL, 2006).

9. Thayer, Accordance Bible Software, (Altamonte Springs, FL, 2006). The participle "anxiously" is formed from a Greek verb that means "to cause intense pain." Joseph and Mary had been in anguish for several days and felt their Son was the root cause of their great anxiety.

10. Saint Augustine, City of God, Translated by Gerald G. Walsh, S.J; Demetrius B. Zema, S.J.; Grace Monahan, O.S.U.; Daniel J. Honan. Edited and abridged by

Vernon J. Bourke, (New York, NY, Image Books Doubleday, 1958) p. 456.

11. Ibid., p. 460.

....

Chapter 5 Endnotes

1. Soteriology is the doctrine of salvation; eschatology is the doctrine of last things.

2. Louw and Nida, Accordance Bible Software, (Altamonte Springs, FL, 2006).

3. Theological Dictionary of the New Testament, Accordance Bible Software, (Altamonte Springs, FL, 2006).

4. The asterisk in the NAS translation of the New Testament denotes the use of a grammatical vehicle known as a "historical present." It is the use of the present tense to speak of a past event, for the purpose of vividly bringing the reader, as it were, into the actual event the author is describing.

5. John MacArthur, The MacArthur Study Bible, (Nashville, TN, Word Publishing, 1997). Commentary on John 13:1.

6. The noun "love" in 1 Peter 4:8 is the familiar New Testament term "agape." It is the noun form of the verb used in John 1:13 to describe the perfect love with which Christ loved His disciples. It is also the same terminology used to describe the love with which the Father loves the Son and all believers. It is this love that God puts into the heart of Christians making it possible for them to express this glorious virtue to others (John 17:20, 23, 26; Romans 5:5).

7. See footnote #4

8. J. C. Ryle, The Duties of Parents, edited by Marcelo A. Tolopilo, Chart & Compass Press, 2008. First published in 1888, London, England.

9. "Road-Reading" start up list:

Fictional Works
Keeper of the Bees, by Gene Stratton-Porter
Teddy's Button, by Amy LeFeuvre (Lamplighter Classic)
Joel a Boy of Galilee, by Annie Fellows Johnston (Lamplighter Classic)
Treasures of the Snow, by Patricia St. John
Tom Sawyer, by Mark Twain

Biographies and Historical Eras
Through Many Dangers, The Story of John Newton, by Brian H. Edwards
Hudson Taylor & Maria, by John Pollock
The Hiding Place, by John & Elizabeth Sherrill
Uncle Tom's Cabin, by Harriet Beecher Stowe
Six Days of War ('67 Arab/Israeli war), by Michael B. Oren
Of Plymouth Plantation, by William Bradford

....

Chapter 7 Endnotes

1. Retrieved from http://www.goldengatebridge.org (February 14, 2008)

2. Wall Street Journal. (January 4, 2006). Retrieved from http://www.Imapactlab.com/.

3. Schlafly, Phyllis, NEA Agenda is Frightening to Parents (July 26, 2006). Retrieved from http://www.Eagleforum.org/.

4. This discussion harkens back to chapters 3 and 6, and two of the most focused battlegrounds in the war against the family - the undermining of the parent/child relationship, and the moral compromise of children.

5. Brave New Schools, Charges Dropped Against Jailed Dad (author unspecified) (October 20, 2005). Retrieved from http://www.WorldNetDaily.com/

6. Morson, Berny, Bill Would Create Sex-ed Standards (April 5, 2007). Retrieved from http://www.rockymountainnews.com/.

7. Unruh, Bob, Principal Bans Parents from Pro-'Gay' Seminar – Public District Students Offered Guidance on Being Homosexual (February 8, 2008). Retrieved from http://www.worldnetdaily.com/.

8. Unruh, Bob, 'Mom' and 'Dad' Banished from California – Schwarzenegger Signs Law Outlawing Terms Perceived as Negative to 'Gays' (February 8, 2008). Retrieved from http://www.worldnetdaily.com/.

....

Chapter 8 Endnotes

1. New Testament term for all believers meaning "holy ones."

Duties of Parents Endnotes

1. As a minister, I cannot help remarking that there is hardly any subject about which people seem so tenacious, as they are about their children. I have sometimes been perfectly astonished at the slowness of sensible Christian parents to allow that their own children are in fault, or deserve blame. There are not a few persons to whom I would far rather speak about their own sins, than tell them their children had done anything wrong.

2. (Editor's note) A stone for sharpening tools

3. "He has seen but little of life who does not discern everywhere the effect of education on men's opinions and habits of thinking. The children bring out of the nursery that which displays itself throughout their lives." -Cecil.

4. As to the age when the biblical instruction of a child should begin, no general rule can be laid down. The mind seems to open in some children much more quickly than in others. We seldom begin too early. There are wonderful examples on record of what a child can attain to, even at three years old.

5. (Editor's note) The God given means for those of us who are in the church to grow in Christ and in love toward one another: fellowship, hearing of the Word, worship, service, the Lord's table, etc.

6. (Editor's note) Pastor Ryle's paraphrase of the remainder of the verse.

7. (Editor's note) "Honor your father and your mother, that your days may be long in the land that the LORD your God is giving you" Exodus 20:12.

8. Some parents and nurses have a way of saying, "Naughty child," to a boy or girl on every slight occasion, and often without good cause. It is a very foolish habit. Words of blame should never be used without real reason.

9. As to the best way of punishing a child, no general rule can be laid down. The characters of children are so exceedingly different, that what would be a severe punishment to one child, would be no punishment at all to another. I only beg to enter my decided protest against the modern notion that no child ought ever to be spanked. Doubtless some parents use bodily correction far too much, and far too violently; but many others, I fear, use it far too little.

To order additional copies of this book:

Email Orders: orders@witp.org

Postal Orders: Walking In The Promises
P.O. Box 890385
Temecula, CA 92589-0385

Website Orders: www.witp.org

Walking In The Promises invites you to host our...

Family conference:
"God's Passion and Provision for Your Family"

Homeschool mothers' conference:
"Recapturing the Joy of Home Education, A Conference to Refresh the Hearts of Homeschool Moms."

For more information, please inquire at:
info@witp.org OR www.witp.org